00-2073

00-2073

COLLECTOR'S ENCYCLOPEDIA
of

POTTERY

IDENTIFICATION & VALUES

DARLENE HURST DOMMEL

COLLECTOR BOOKS
A Division of Schroeder Publishing Co., Inc.

The current values in this book should be used only as a guide. They are not intended to set prices, which vary from one section of the country to another. Auction prices as well as dealer prices vary greatly and are affected by condition as well as demand. Neither the author nor the publisher assumes responsibility for any losses that might be incurred as a result of consulting this guide.

ON THE COVER

Prairie rose spoon rest, $75.00 – 100.00; bison figurine, $300.00 – 400.00; pheasant salt and pepper shakers, $35.00 – 45.00 pair; swirl vase, $200.00 – 300.00.

SEARCHING FOR A PUBLISHER?

We are always looking for knowledgeable people considered to be experts within their fields. If you feel that there is a real need for a book on your collectible subject and have a large comprehensive collection, contact Collector Books.

Cover photograph: Peter Lee
Cover design: Beth Summers
Book design: Karen Geary

COLLECTOR BOOKS
P.O. Box 3009
Paducah, KY 42002-3009
http://www.collectorbooks.com

Copyright © 2000 by Darlene Hurst Dommel

CONTENTS

ACKNOWLEDGMENTS

This book is dedicated to the Rosemeade pottery collectors and former employees who generously shared knowledge, loaned archival photographs, submitted pricing information, and allowed personal collections to be photographed. Their unselfish support ensured that Rosemeade pottery, which reflects the spirit of the people and the land, would receive its deserved recognition.

Collectors and Supporters:
George and Lorraine Williams
Virgil and Dianne Bohn
Brad Bird
Arley and Bonnie Olson
Oz and Ardeen Sveum
Ray and Marlene Koble
Manville and Alice Stoltenow
Dale and Janice Deike
Con and Sandy Short
Jim Norine
Don Lawrence
Dr. Marion Nelson
Fran Vasicek
Bill and Laurie Vasicek
AW and Beth Hill
Bob and Jan Barr
Otto and Mary Bang
Rita Lewis Carew
Curt Rustand
Dan Ludemann
Ken Metzen
Quentin Christman
Steve Schoneck
Ervin and Janice Hanson
Gary and Kandi Mitchell
Gene Roesler
Jack Kennedy
Burdell and Doris Hall

Former Employees:
Joe and Betty McLaughlin
Warren and Margie Olson
Darel and Milli Stanley
Olga Hektner
Marie Connelly
Lyle Mitzell
Emma Althoff
Violet Radeke
Pearl Kackman
The late Howard Lewis

Members of the North Dakota Pottery Collectors Society formed the backbone of this group. Due to time and other constraints, I was unable to visit all those who offered to contribute information and photographs of their collections.

I want especially to thank my husband, Jim, my photographer, supporter, and consultant. Thanks to Diann Dommel Honadel for her editorial expertise, Christine Dommel Keating and Diann for their computer assistance, and David Dommel for artistic advice.

The staff and volunteers of the Richland County Historical Museum, Chester Fritz Library, State Historical Society of North Dakota, American Wildlife Art Galleries, and Bill Bakken's *Rosemeade Price Guide* (517-26th St. NW, Rochester, MN 55901) provided valuable resources.

I am also grateful to my editor, Lisa Stroup, and the Collector Books staff.

PREFACE

Hopefully, this book will stimulate further research, study, and preservation of Rosemeade pottery pieces. Although an extensive array of Rosemeade products are included, any book is only a progress report. New information will surface, new shapes will be found, new glaze colors described. Perception of pieces will change. The continuing quest for additional knowledge makes collecting vital and alive.

Precise, detailed records were not kept by the company. As the North Dakota Pottery Collectors Society membership information states, "No records have been found listing all the items that were produced. As someone adds a unique find to their collection and shares it with others, our knowledge grows."

Many early pieces, both swirl and other, were hand thrown. Hand-thrown swirl pieces continued to be made later. A complete listing of all hand-thrown objects is impossible as each individual piece is different. Others were made as one-of-a-kind "lunch hour" or special pieces.

Whenever possible, terminology used in this book is that taken from company advertising or company promotional materials, although common usage by collectors may be different. The use of company product names and glaze colors, taken from stock listings, advertisements, invoices, and promotions, helps avoid confusion.

The terms ashtrays, spoon rests, and pin trays were used interchangeably in company stock lists, probably to increase marketability as multiple purpose products. Collectors also do not always agree whether specific items are ashtrays, spoon rests, or pin trays. Therefore, the designations ashtrays, spoon rests, and pin trays may be used interchangeably in this book.

Most salt and pepper shakers were also made as figurines. However, they may not always be listed.

Shapes are repeated occasionally to show different colors. Because of the rarity of Rosemeade jewelry, many colors and variations were photographed.

Pieces or colors noted as available have been seen by the author or documented in company literature. Other pieces or colors may also be found.

Mold variations and production techniques make all measurements approximate. Company measurements are used when possible. Measurements are listed as height-width-length if three dimensions are included. Two dimensions are given with height first, followed by width or length. One dimension denotes the most significant to that object — height, width, length, or diameter.

Prices, based on mint condition, are only a guide, providing a general overview of scarcity and quality. Rarity is difficult to determine, but some items considered rare are so marked. One-of-a-kind and extremely rare pieces are not priced since they seldom appear on the market.

This book includes excerpts from the author's books, *Collector's Encyclopedia of the Dakota Potteries* and *Collector's Encyclopedia of Howard Pierce Porcelain*, both published by Collector Books.

HISTORY

Rosemeade — descriptive tradename for a popular North Dakota pottery — instills images of the state flower, the wild prairie rose. Fragrant wild prairie roses, their profuse colorful blossoms growing thickly in the meadows, brightening the unbounded prairies, have become treasured by North Dakotans as their state flower. Laura Taylor, the creator of Rosemeade pottery, was born in Rosemeade township, named after the Norwegian hometown of an early settler. "When the first pioneers set foot upon this land, the Prairie Rose must have welcomed them with its modest blush and must have brought many a home-hunger to the wanderer."[1]

Prairie rose trademark

Laura Taylor, growing up in a rural North Dakota home, attended a country one-room school through eighth grade. Since education was a priority of the early pioneers, country schools were established by townships for farm children. As Laura walked the mile to and from school every day, she walked through "the wide-open space where wild roses grow."[2] A mead (meadow) of roses "tinted the landscape and filled the air with its delicate fragrance."[3]

After graduating from Valley City State University, Laura Taylor taught in a country school. When Laura's students asked to do art projects, Laura was dismayed as she knew nothing about the subject. That next summer, Laura Taylor enrolled at Valley City Teacher's College to learn drawing and modeling, the beginning of a whole new world. Delighted with her first imperfect clay sculpture, a kangaroo, Laura taught her students to make "vases and clumsy animals." Their eyes would "shine with joy as they chuckled over their handwork."[4]

During a summer term, Laura Taylor enrolled in a clay molding course taught by Glen Lukens, visiting California professor and nationally-known studio potter. Laura discovered that, "There was something very remarkable and satisfying in taking a piece of plaster clay, shaping it and finally taking the finished article, shining and beautiful, from the kiln."[5]

The "enthusiasm and influence" of her inspiring teacher "made a lasting impression."[6] "I recognized this to be a work which I wanted to do. I was interested in making pottery not as a hobby, but as a means of earning a living."[7]

Having chosen pottery making as a career, Laura went to the University of North Dakota in 1932, where she took arts and ceramics classes for three years. During 1933 to 1934, Professor W.M. Budge employed her as a part-time assistant in the ceramic department making pottery to sell. "I designed a few pottery figurines, made the plaster molds, cast, finished and glazed them."[8] This was Laura's "first practical experience using a commercial method. Without the kind interest and encouragement of Mr. Budge I would probably not have been able to continue my ceramic education to the point where I had enough practical knowledge to start my own pottery."[9]

At UND, Laura Taylor started out making items from molds made by others, like Director Margaret Cable. However, Laura was soon creating her own models, making molds from these models and then casting and painting pieces. Learning and perfecting all these processes were essential training for Laura's later work at Rosemeade. As Laura Taylor watched her demonstrate on the wheel, instructor Julia Mattson recalled, "When Laura saw the whirling lump of clay emerge as a hollow and graceful vase, she burst out laughing in sheer astonishment and delight."[10]

UND documentation shows that Laura Taylor created several items for sale at UND. These included Native American head and bison bookends; coyote, gopher, frog, rabbit, and rooster paperweights; wild rose, crocus, and pasque flower tiles; small and large flickertail and bison plaques; and bison heads. Her ashtrays included wheat, Native American, bison, coyote, frog, and cactus motifs. Prices ranged from fifty cents for the bentonite cactus ashtray to five dollars for the bison heads. Freida Hammers, a UND instructor, described Laura's work as "naturalistic." She had a natural flair for modeling."[11]

Genie lamp with prairie rose motif made by Laura Taylor at the University of North Dakota for the Minot Art Club.

Early recognition for Laura Taylor came with a UND mosaic tile plaque exhibited in the North Dakota building at the 1933 Chicago Century of Progress World's Fair. Laura Taylor's plaque was displayed in a series of eleven picture plaques showing major North Dakota industries. Taylor created the design while she was a student in the UND art department and then completed the plaque as an assistant in the ceramic department.

A 1933 newspaper clipping tells of a clay lion sculpture presented by the Bismarck Lions Club to the International Lions Club president, "Everyone who sees it not only appreciates the fact that it is a lion, with

all of its symbolic meaning, but that it is a rare work of art and reflects the skillful technique of Miss Laura Taylor of the ceramics department at the University of North Dakota."[12]

After Laura Taylor returned to teaching for a year in Menoken, UND professor William Budge again influenced her life. Budge was instrumental in bringing the Works Progress Administration Federal Arts Project to North Dakota. During the Great Depression, President Franklin Roosevelt proposed a social and economic program, the Works Progress Administration (WPA), as part of his New Deal federal programs. One branch of the WPA, the Federal Arts Project (FAP), served the following three purposes: helping professional artists, training non-artists to make a living working with ceramics, and providing crafts instruction in communities. In 1936, Professor Budge, WPA statewide project director, appointed Laura Taylor state supervisor of the North Dakota WPA/FAP, headquartered first in Dickinson and later in Mandan.

The ceramics project blossomed under Laura Taylor's direction as she trained the workers and supervised the making of pottery which was given to schools and government institutions throughout the state. "Out of a melee of clay, plaster of Paris models, manicure tools and ingenuity come rows and rows of vases, pitchers, bowls, and novelties."[13] Eleven staff women without clay work experience "have displayed unusual ability in designing and modeling...Its object, to train otherwise unemployed individuals to earn their own livelihood

"Flock of Sheep on the Range," Laura Taylor's mosaic tile plaque exhibited at the 1933 Century of Progress World's Fair in Chicago, Illinois, 1933.

(Ceramics Department photograph courtesy of the Elwyn B. Robinson Department of Special Collections, University of North Dakota.)

LEFT:
Ashtray designed by Laura Taylor at the Dickinson Clay Products Company.

RIGHT:
Mark on bottom of Dickota ashtray.

and to discover hidden talent, has been more than fulfilled."[14] Afternoon classes in modeling were also offered, "with ten women in the city now being instructed by Miss Taylor."[15]

While the WPA program was in Dickinson, all WPA glazing and firing was done at the Dickinson Clay Products Company. Some WPA workers became employees of the Dickinson Company. The *Dickinson Press* newspaper stated that "a number of her (Laura Taylor) models which are being used by the Dickinson Clay Products Company for Dickota pottery have received very favorable response."[16]

A life-changing opportunity arose in 1939 as Laura Taylor was asked to demonstrate pottery making at the World of Tomorrow Exposition in New York City. The New York World's Fair, with its theme of The World of Tomorrow "presented a message of hope and prosperity after a period of grinding depression."[17] International expositions "served cultural, political and economic interests as participating nations used these occasions to present the richness of their achievements in art, architecture and industry."[18]

For six months, Laura Taylor demonstrated throwing on the wheel in the Federal Theatre Building as part of the WPA display. Taylor worked as visitors watched and asked questions. Over and over came the remark, "I bet you made mud pie when you were a little girl."[19]

New York opened new doors for Laura Taylor. She was "able to make a valuable study of the modern pottery which the foreign countries displayed in their building on the fair grounds and...continued my study of ceramics in the numerous museums and art galleries of New York City."[20]

Robert J. Hughes, president of the Greater North Dakota Association and a zealous booster of state enterprise, had previously corresponded with Laura Taylor. Hughes had no experience in pottery manufacture, but was interested in pursuing commercial possibilities for native clay. As Hughes wanted to start his own pottery, Professor Budge recommended Laura Taylor because of her previous pottery experience. Taylor ignored Hughes' letter about starting a pottery in his hometown. Having never met, Robert Hughes watched Laura's World Fair pottery demonstration. Hughes later proposed a business venture over coffee and donuts at a fairground's food stand, and a partnership was formed. Laura Taylor's dream of making pottery "not as a hobby, but as a means of earning a living" was about to come true.[21]

Laura Taylor throwing on wheel, New York World's Fair, 1939.
(Ceramics Department photograph courtesy of the Elwyn B. Robinson Department of Special Collections, University of North Dakota.)

The Wahpeton Pottery Company was founded in January 1940. Robert Hughes, owner of Wahpeton's Globe-Gazette Printing Company and Gift Shop, provided the capital and became president/promoter/business manager. Laura Taylor, partner/secretary/treasurer, provided the creative genius.

A single room in the Masonic building next to the alley of the Globe Gazette Printing Company became the first Rosemeade plant. One kiln was housed in a tin shed behind the building. Left-over equipment had been purchased after the demise of the Dickinson Clay Products Company. Other "equipment consisted of a handmade clay mixer, two wash tubs and some jars and shelves."[22]

Founding a pottery company was a huge gamble. "With more enthusiasm than experience, we started out. Persons who knew more about the business would have probably been afraid of the pit falls and not dared to risk the money it took to start in even a small way."[23] Taylor's personal papers also show that she recognized "ceramics as a competitive field," and the problem of "not knowing what people like."[24]

The state capitol of North Dakota became Laura Taylor's choice for the first piece of pottery made by the newly formed company. Her rendition of the capitol, a slender skyscraper shaft jutting starkly from the prairies of Bismarck, celebrated its unusual architecture. Demolished by a spectacular fire in 1930, the original capitol was replaced with a contemporary structure, "constructed almost entirely of North Dakota brick, stone and tile,"[25] boasted the Greater North Dakota Association, a group dedicated to promoting North Dakota products. Described as a "daring design" erected in 1934, "majestic limestone walls tower nineteen stories over the wide-flung legislature wing,"[26] with an Art Deco interior. Laura Hughes later described this piece as taking "the most painstaking work of any which I have ever made."[27]

Laura Taylor created a small model of The Chahinkapa Park Visitor's Register as her second piece of pottery for the Wahpeton Pottery Company. This souvenir version was given by the Globe-Gazette Printing Company. The register, publicized as the world's largest record book, is 33" high, 58" wide, 9½"

North Dakota state capitol

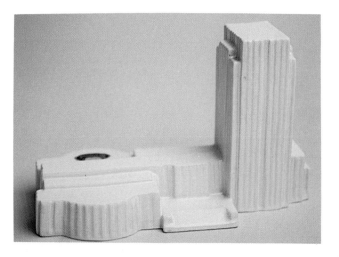

Rare model of state capitol, 4½" x 7¾", $2,000.00+.

Rare Rosemeade souvenir version of Chahinkapa Park Register, ½" x 2½" x 4½", text on the back described the huge volume, $400.00+.

thick and weighs 507 pounds. When open, it has a 113" "wing span" and provides space for more than 760,000 signatures. While chairman of the City Park Committee, Robert Hughes conceived the park promotion idea, to be manufactured by his Globe-Gazette Printing Company. The Visitor's Register is still being used by the Richland County Historical Museum.

Laura Taylor's other early designs also reflected North Dakota. She described early products as "western, representing our own state, flower vases and jardinieres in wild rose and wheat designs, coyotes, and ashtrays with Indian heads, cowboys and wheat."[28]

Inviting the general public "to visit the plant and inspect this fascinating manufacturing process, one of the oldest in the modern world today,"[29] the Wahpeton Pottery Company announced an open house in October 1940. The local newspaper indicated that "a beautiful little pottery souvenir will be presented to the lady visitors on opening day."[30]

Nearly a thousand visitors attended the open house, with seven hundred souvenirs presented to women. The pottery plaque, a horseshoe "WISH US GOOD LUCK" surrounding a bowl of prairie roses was inscribed on the back "OPEN HOUSE OCT. 18 – 1940 WAHPETON POTTERY CO. Rosemeade."

When the company started, Laura Taylor did most of the work herself. Soon the Wahpeton Pottery Company became a five-person enterprise with a new wooden facility built in August 1940. Vera Gethman, from Gorham, North Dakota, joined the staff as a design artist. According to a company brochure, Gethman modeled small naturalistic animal figurines, especially horses, using living models. About two hundred pieces were made the first year.

By January 1941, eleven people were employed. Newspaper accounts in 1943 describe twenty employees ranging in age from their teens to the seventies. Weekly production resulted in 1,900 salt and pepper shakers and 4,500 other products.

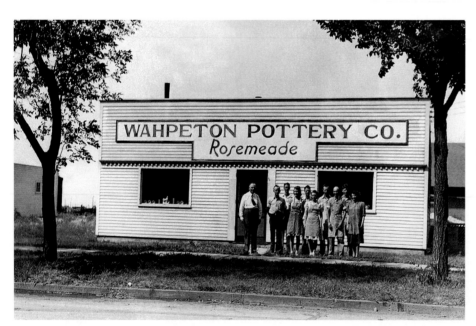

Original building of the Wahpeton Pottery Company and early employees.
(Courtesy of State Historical Society of North Dakota.)

LEFT:
Open house bisque souvenir of prairie rose bouquet within a horseshoe, ¼" x 2" x 2", front of horseshoe states "WISH US GOOD LUCK W. P. CO.," $1,200.00+.

RIGHT:
Back of open house souvenir states "OPEN HOUSE OCT 18 – 1940 WAHPETON POTTERY CO. ROSEMEADE." Some were fired to a darker color.

Before the World War II, items such as figurines, salt and pepper shakers, and wall pockets were being produced in Japan and sold in the United States. With the onset of the war, Japanese imports ceased and American potteries successfully filled this void.

During the war years, several conditions made operating the pottery difficult. Trained employees left for the armed services or defense plant work. "Since we started the plant I (Laura Taylor) have been at different times the finisher, glazer, mold maker. Now from necessity I became the kiln setter as well, crawling into the kiln to set the heavy shelves in place and put the pots on them."[31]

New pottery equipment was not manufactured, preventing expansion of the pottery. Even replacements for repair were hard to obtain. "Glaze materials, such as tin and uranium could not be purchased as they were critical materials needed by the government. We had done a great deal of experimental work with glazes when we first worked out our glaze formulas. Now we had to change the formulas and replace their critical materials with others."[32] For example, the supply of uranium oxide, "used in compounding the glossy red glaze which adorns the head and breast of the pheasant"[33] ceased as it was used in the atomic bomb. However, Laura continued, "These things are merely inconveniences, such as occurred in all lines of endeavor during these trying times. We kept our plant running and our pottery was well received wherever it was sold."[34]

Clay and romance intermingled with time. In 1942, five young Rosemeade women employees became brides and "this matrimonial contagion spread into the executive offices."[35] This time, Robert Hughes proposed marriage to Laura Taylor, and their business relationship expanded into a marital one in 1943.

Howard Lewis, welcomed as a partner and production manager of the Wahpeton Pottery Company in 1944, expanded the company horizons. Lewis' excellent background as a ceramic engineer and expert technician, along with experience at six previous potteries, led to the formation of new glazes and development of new products for Rosemeade.

As a ceramic engineering student at Iowa State College, Lewis had studied with Paul Cox, a well-known ceramic chemist who created Newcomb College's famous soft matt glaze. Paul Cox enabled Lewis to complete his college education by hiring him as a stu-

dent to rebuild their kiln and develop Iowa clay deposits. Lewis was the only member of his ceramic class to get a job upon college graduation in 1932. At the Niloak Pottery Company, Benton, Arkansas, Lewis developed new glazes and clay mixtures for the Hywood line. A periodical of the time described him as a persistent hard worker, who "prefers the practical application of his knowledge on a commercial scale to the pursuit of theory,"[36] a preference demonstrated repeatedly in his life.

Laura Taylor Hughes had previously worked with Howard Lewis, Dickinson Clay Products Company superintendent. Mr. Hughes

Howard Lewis, partner and production manager in 1945.

was also familiar with Lewis' work and had contacted him regarding starting a Wahpeton pottery while Lewis worked at the Mason City Brickyards. With their company expanding, both husband and wife recognized the need for Howard Lewis' creative innovation and expertise. They persuaded him to leave the Tycer Pottery Company, Roseville, Ohio, and join them.

This trio formed the "perfect combination to ensure success. Mr. Hughes brought business and marketing knowledge, plus financial resources, that combined with the artistry of Mrs. Hughes, and the production know how of Mr. Lewis guaranteed the vitality of the entire enterprise."[37]

A cinder block fireproof expansion to house the kilns was added to the rear of the wooden building in 1944. Because a modern production plant was necessary two years later, a brick building expansion was completed.

At peak capacity, during the early 1950s, twenty-seven employees were producing 1,400 pieces daily. The 165 different items produced by the Wahpeton Pottery Company in 1948 now reached over 250 designs, with a diverse variety of products.

Although several employees mentioned low wages, the loyal employees took pride in their work.

Company building with brick expansion.

One employee stated, "I didn't call it work. I wasn't tired when the day ended."[38] Another employee told of noon potlucks and spontaneous "sing-alongs" when working. The employees worked together closely and became friends. Laura Taylor Hughes promoted good labor-management relationships and stimulated creativity by encouraging employee participation. Workers often had ideas for new designs or new details for old designs. A newspaper article noted that, "When a new item is being produced, the factory teems with excitement and the employees are the first ones to buy the new pieces."[39] Employee turnover was extremely low, with a waiting list of job applicants.

Annual company Christmas parties were usually held at the Hughes' home or sometimes at local restaurants. An employee scrapbook stated, "At our Christmas parties we each received a card with generous bonus check enclosed."[40]

Rosemeade pottery became popular for Christmas gifts. For example, a 1952 local newspaper noted that Bambi deer figurines (page 108) had excellent sales during the holidays, along with song birds and game birds native to the area. Company correspondence described Rosemeade Christmas gifts, such as pheasants in 1947, given to state officials by the Hughes.

Laura Taylor Hughes' papers indicate that one year Dalmatian dog heads were given as Christmas gifts from the Wahpeton Pottery Company." In the good old days these coach dogs accompanied the carriage when holiday guests arrived and added gaiety to the festive scene with their handsome spotted coats. Today as part of our Rosemeade family of twelve dogs they bring you our cheeriest Christmas Greetings."[41]

Many sources indicated that the company was not a strictly disciplined operation. Work rules are not evident. Even if any rules were laid down, employees would not follow them. Supervision was inconsistent. Several employees stated that management personnel seldom came to their work areas. The management style could be described as laissez-faire, which one would expect in a small town, family-style operation.

Hazel Lewis, Howard Lewis, Laura Taylor Hughes, and Robert Hughes.

All the female Rosemeade employees wearing sunbonnets for Wahpeton's 80th Celebration.

All the male employees, some in hats and ties for the Wahpeton 80th Celebration.

Rosemeade parade float with Linda Cummins, daughter of Cliff and Elaine Cummins, and Karen Olson, daughter of Warren and Margie Olson, in the vases.

For example, stories abound regarding the misuse of Rosemeade bisque ware. An employee brought home ceramic pheasants, which neighborhood boys used for target practice with BB guns. Another employee brought a child's wagon full of bisque ware to a neighbor woman who placed the pieces all over her garden. Employees tell of playing catch with pieces at the factory, which would sail from one end of the room to another.

In a letter to an artist seeking a job at the pottery in 1951, Laura Taylor wrote about Rosemeade's unskilled labor. "Most of our work must necessarily be done by unskilled labor and we get the effects we want by having the original models which I make worked out very much in detail. No original work is required by the employees." [42] Thus, Taylor informed the artist that the Wahpeton Pottery Company was unable to consider her for employment. Employees described being trained on the job, often by each other.

"A farm girl who at an early age fell in love with the native flowers, birds, animals, and scenes of North Dakota," [43] Laura Taylor Hughes' inspirations were many. Laura worked from real life whenever possible, "with nature regarded as the ultimate source book for design inspiration." [44] She also used sketches, pictures, clippings, booklets, and mounted animals and birds. Her holdings related closely to her work. For example, Laura's personal papers include thick folders of pictures illustrating pheasants, Egyptian motifs, etc.

In a 1950 letter, Laura Hughes described her process of creating a new item. "I have collected pictures on many subjects to use as reference material. If I wish to design a fawn for instance, I get out my file of pictures on fawns, take a lump of damp clay and set to work. I do most of the work while the clay is fairly damp and pliable so that I may turn legs and head in different positions to study the effect." [45]

On trips across the United States, Laura chatted with dealers, getting their ideas for new designs. On her worldwide travels, Laura was constantly collecting ideas and reference materials including actual pottery pieces.

Perusal of Laura Taylor Hughes' personal collection of examples from other potteries shows that some of the same techniques and shapes were also used for Rosemeade pottery. For instance, a Czechoslovakian sailboat, Rookwood bud vase, and Van Briggle vase closely resemble Rosemeade products. "The design for a little matt green vase is taken almost directly from

"Molded stylized plant forms under a slightly mottled green matt glaze," as described by Marion Nelson in *Art Pottery of the Midwest*. 4⅝" x 3" vase, with Rosemeade ink stamp, design similar to the Amaryllis line of Brush-McCoy Pottery.

the Amaryllis line of Ohio's Brush-McCoy produced in the 1920s, which was, in turn, a late manifestation of Grueby's design principles from two decades earlier." [46]

According to Martin Eidelberg, art historian, already at the turn of the century American ceramists "not only admired but also imitated their European colleagues' works...Our histories are intertwined and mutually illuminating." [47] Ellsworth Woodward of Newcomb Pottery stated, "In the shape of vases it is not possible to avoid imitation, the best forms having been for centuries established." [48]

So also, Rosemeade artisans used proven techniques and shapes and then moved forward in their creative endeavors. After "an initial impetus to move in the direction (of nature-based forms), nature provided gifted ceramists with an unlimited repertoire of ideas." [49]

Laura Taylor Hughes had the ability to determine mass market appeal and then create saleable designs for that market. "I find that people like to know what they are looking at. It is I think quite doubtful if they would buy it unless they knew what it was. From necessity, then, and also because it is the way I like to do it, when designing pottery I make birds and animals recognizable. This seems to be what the American people want so I guess we will go right on making it." [50]

Also an astute observer of trends, Laura met the needs and wishes of the public. This is why her company remained successful while many other pottery companies of that era did not survive the tough times. For example, several Rosemeade designs were inspired by a flower arranging craze which swept across England and this country in the 1950s. "Each year sees more clubs form and more ladies take up the art. It is extremely stimulating for the creative woman ...it will satisfy her sense of the dramatic," noted a national magazine. "Manufacturers sought to match these creative and dramatic urges with suitably inventive receptacles."[51]

Rosemeade pottery floral arrangement products.

Laura Taylor captured the essence of North Dakota in several Rosemeade pottery renditions of state symbols. "State symbols remind us of who we are, our history, the way we live, and the beauty of our state. Symbols are often a focal point for the pride we feel in North Dakota."[52] The wild prairie rose which is the state flower was chosen in 1907. This rose was honored by use in the company tradename, as previously discussed.

The western meadowlark, North Dakota's 1947 official state bird, appears on various Rosemeade items from plaques to pins. Montana, Wyoming, Nebraska and Oregon also honor the western meadowlark as their state bird.

As the clear flute-like song of this gregarious bird echoes across the prairie landscape, memories stir for many North Dakotans. Theodore Roosevelt in 1883 expressed his thought of the meadowlark's melodious song, "sometimes with a cadence of wild sadness, inexpressibly touching....It comes forever laden with a hundred memories and associations, with the sight of dim hills reddening in the dawn, with the breath of cool morning winds blowing across lonely plains, with the scent of flowers on the sunlit prairie, with the motion of fiery horses, with the strong thrill of eager and buoyant life."[53]

A living monument to peace, the International Peace Garden near Bottineau demonstrates that two nations can and do live in harmony along the world's longest unfortified boundary. Straddling the Canadian–United States border, the 2,339-acre botanical symbol of peace was dedicated in 1932 as a tribute to friendship between the people of Canada and the United States. "The Peace Garden State," North Dakota's nickname, was formally adopted in 1957. This slogan appears on many Rosemeade ashtrays and other products.

North Dakota gets its nickname "Flickertail State" from the Richardson ground squirrels, the flickertails, which are abundant in North Dakota. The flickertail is a tiny, agile rodent which gets its name from "spontaneously switching its tail, usually with a final upward flip" when danger approaches.[54]

LEFT:
Extremely rare 5¾" western meadowlark plaque.

RIGHT:
Extremely rare 5¾" flickertail plaque.

The northern pike was designated North Dakota's fish in 1969. Considered an outstanding, tasty game fish, the northern pike appears on several Rosemeade products.

By identifying special niches of interest and creating items for specific regions, organizations, and places, the company generated several marketing successes. Examples demonstrate the national scope of production. Although initially made for special sales in their native areas, most found "generally large sales throughout the country."[55]

Turkeys were made for the National Turkey Federation, pandas for Chicago's Brookfield Zoo, Rocky Mountain goats and bears for Glacier National Park, and tulips for Holland, Michigan. Several items illustrated state themes, like alligators and flamingos for Florida, quail for Georgia, and mules for Missouri. State symbols were also manufactured, including the golden poppy, state flower of California; sunflower, state flower of Kansas; pelican, state bird of Louisiana; and the popular pheasant, state bird of South Dakota.

"Great Northern Railway" seal on mountain goat plaque.

Several designs were created for the neighboring state of Minnesota. Laura stated, "Our Minnesota dealers requested mallards so I made these."[56] "Fish on a platter in a variety which included the principal freshwater game fish (walleye) proved popular with sportsmen, particularly visitors in the Minnesota resort area."[57] Other items directed to the Minnesota market included Paul Bunyan and Babe, the Indian God of Peace, the ladyslipper (state flower) and the gopher, (state animal).

After being sold first only at the factory, sales of Rosemeade expanded to the Chahinkapa Park Souvenir Shop, Wahpeton by early spring of 1940. A downtown sales room next to the Globe Gazette later opened.

By December 1940, thirty dealers in the northwest were handling Rosemeade pottery. Rosemeade was soon marketed heavily in the upper Midwest. Two-thirds of all 1943 sales were in North and South Dakota, Minnesota, Iowa, Wisconsin, Nebraska, and Montana. Marketing eventually expanded to include most states in the Union. Traveling sales representatives were recruited throughout the country as these *The Gift and Art Buyer* advertisements indicate: "TRAVELING SALESMAN wanted to sell Rosemeade Giftware, a quality pottery to Gift and Department stores in Kansas and Missouri,"[58] in the June 1949 issue. An August 1950 ad stated, "SALESMAN WANTED to cover New England states with Rosemeade line of pottery giftware. Must make regular calls on the trade."[59] Other ads sought salesmen in the territory of New York, Pennsylvania, New Jersey, and the Kentucky-Tennessee territory.

Rosemeade products were sold by the department stores of Marshall Field and Company and Carson Pirie Scott and Company of Chicago, and the Dayton Company of Minneapolis. Tourist destinations including the Museum of Science and Industry in Chicago and the American Museum of National History in New York City placed repeated orders. Several national parks, like the Grand Canyon, Yellowstone, and Glacier, carried Rosemeade souvenirs.

Rosemeade products were being marketed in foreign countries by 1953. A local newspaper showed Rosemeade employees packing a couple dozen snack trays with chicken pick holders for shipment to South Africa.

Rosemeade advertisements appeared regularly in trade magazines like *The Gift and Art Buyer*, *Giftwares*, and *The Retail Tobacconist* in the late 1940s and early 1950s. Other promotions highlighted new products.

Mass merchandising through an undated Sears Roebuck catalog advertisement offered two-inch quail and pheasant pairs of salt and pepper shakers sold for $2.89 a set. The description stated, "made of highly glazed pottery, with natural coloring and fine detail, two pairs that are charming for your table and a delight to collectors."[60]

Rosemeade Giftware
Salt and Peppers

This pair of bantams introduces our unusual line of salt and pepper sets all well designed, beautifully glazed and moderately priced. There are wild life numbers in birds, animals and fish, as well as novelty items in cacti, Dutch windmills with plastic sails and Paul Bunyan with his blue ox.

Illustrated bantam set 60c

Glazed in seven different color combinations including black and white.

Dealers—Write for complete information.

Rosemeade Potteries
Wahpeton, North Dakota

Rosemeade salt and pepper shakers advertisement in January, 1953 *Giftware* magazine.

EGYPTIAN designs highlight the new Rosemeade line of planters, jardinieres, and vases made by the Wahpeton Pottery Co., Wahpeton, N. D. Lined with porous bisque, items have an antique glazed finish in grey or green with black base. Jardinieres, 5 inches high, $4.50 a pair net; vases, 8 inches high, $4.50 a pair net; wall vases, 5½ inches high, $3.60 a pair net.

THE GIFT AND ART BUYER

Promotion of new Rosemeade Egyptian line in *The Gift and Art Buyer*, May, 1950 issue.

The company generated sales tools for their salesmen and dealers. Company brochures described products (Appendix I). Rosemeade Potteries gave promotional ashtrays.

Dealers' signs, with the Rosemeade trademark were made out of pottery and paper. These signs bring together an attention-getting logo, outstanding design, and wonderful colors in a small format to attract the buying public.

Laura Taylor Hughes created interest in Rosemeade ware by giving many speeches to church groups, women's clubs, and community organizations. She showed at several state exhibitions and appeared in a tourist promotion film, "Changing North Dakota." The company provided favors for many banquets like the

Rosemeade Potteries used its popular 5" ashtray as a souvenir of the company, $75.00 – 100.00.

Laura Taylor Hughes exhibited with Ida Bisek Prokop, well-known North Dakota sculptress and artist, at shows like this North Dakota Winter Show in Valley City, North Dakota, April 1943.

Rare dealer signs – 3¾" x 7" with glossy prairie roses; 3¾" x 7¼" with matt prairie roses. $1,500.00+ each.

Rare blue dealer sign, 3¾" x 7", $1,500.00+.

Rare pink dealer sign, 3¾" x 7", $1,500.00+.

local Daughters of the American Revolution (DAR) chapter. Groups like Camp Fire, Boy Scouts, Girl Scouts, Homemakers Club, Business Women's Club, and the North Dakota Press Association toured the pottery.

An incentive for *Richland County Farmer-Globe* subscriptions also promoted Rosemeade pottery. "With each full year's subscription paid in advance, your choice of a piece of Rosemeade pottery FREE!"[61]

Laura Taylor Hughes brought national recognition to North Dakota with her Rosemeade ware. The September 1951 *National Geographic Magazine* featured Laura Hughes in a full-page color photo. With a circulation of over two million at the time, the magazine gave North Dakota and the Wahpeton Pottery Company publicity describing Rosemeade pottery as "one of the most unusual industries" and "a favorite with collectors."[62] Laura Hughes responded, "I think people all over the country will get an entirely new idea of North Dakota."[63]

House Beautiful and *Woman's Day* featured Rosemeade ware in articles. An NBC television show produced in New York City, "The Kathi Norris Show," requested Rosemeade products on a "free promotional basis," The Rosemeade mallard sugar and creamer set

were demonstrated as "novel and practical products of service and interest to viewers" on April 12, 1951, and "televised very beautifully." This TV program also used Rosemeade products as "props" from time to time. "We're very proud to have them on the set."[64]

A 1953 *Fargo Forum* newspaper noted that Laura Hughes "has achieved status not only as a North Dakota artist but as a figure of national significance. Critics praise her deft touch and keen eye for capturing the very feel or essence of the subject."[65]

"Wahpeton Pottery Adorns Nixon Household," a proud local newspaper headline proclaimed. On a 1952 Eisenhower-Nixon presidential campaign tour whistle-stop, Pat Nixon was presented with a pair of large Rosemeade pheasant figurines. *Look* magazine featured the life story of the Vice President's wife in 1954. Pat Nixon was photographed in her sewing rocker, with the pheasants shown decorating their dining room table. When gifts were "deemed fit" to be used in the White House or Vice President's home, "The public found a new sense of respect for these items."[66]

At the 1956 Miss America pageant, Miss North Dakota presented each of the other forty-seven contestants with a peace dove ashtray inscribed with

11" x 8½" paper sign, $20.00 – 30.00.

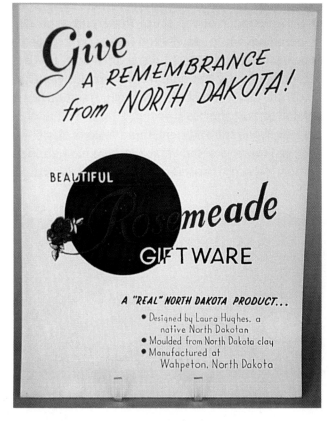

11" x 8½" paper sign, $20.00 – 30.00.

A North Dakota Product - -
"ROSEMEADE" POTTERY
MADE IN NORTH DAKOTA OF
NORTH DAKOTA POTTERY CLAY
Designed by A Native North Dakotan

Paper sign at Richland County Historial Museum.

Paper sign at Richland County Historial Museum.

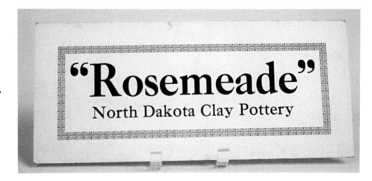

her name. As queen of the Peace Garden State, the gifts were symbolic of the state. These pink ashtrays with perching white doves and the words "North Dakota Peace Garden State" were later sold to the public. However, the first ones from the molds went to the Atlantic City contestants. The gift tradition was continued in 1957 and 1958.

In 1934, while still a student, Laura Taylor's modeled donkey sculpture was shown at the Ceramic National Exhibition, Syracuse Museum of Fine Arts, Syracuse,

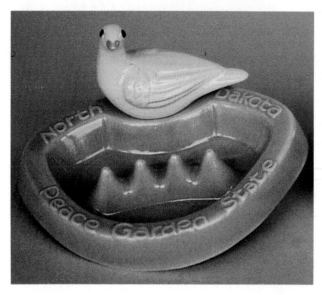

"Dove of Peace" ashtray given to Miss America contestants.

New York, and later sent on tour with their traveling exhibition. Laura was again honored in 1951 when two hand-thrown fish were accepted for the Ceramic Nationals. Because the Ceramic Nationals became a focal point for national recognition in the ceramics field, American ceramists eagerly sought inclusion in the exhibitions. "In consolidating American interest in ceramics, (these exhibitions) provided an experiment station where criteria of quality may be established."[67]

Although Laura Taylor Hughes was known for her naturalistic designs, she could also create award-winning abstract ceramics. Her hand-thrown fanciful modern design fish, accepted for the 1951 Ceramic Nationals, were not a result of "squinting through a spectacle at dead fish or laboring over pictures to get every fin and scale in place. I threw a ball of clay down on the potter's wheel and whipped up each fish which belonged to no particular species."[68] Laura called them "rough fish," glazed in shades of aqua and blue. After Nationals, the fish were part of an exhibit which toured art galleries in several cities, including the University of Minnesota Art Museum in Minneapolis.

Laura Hughes related that, "This is not the first time that pottery which I designed has been displayed in a museum. At the Walker Art Center (an abstract art museum) in Minneapolis, there is a pair of Rosemeade pheasants in a case labeled of all things, 'Bad Art.'"[69] Hughes then pointed out that the American Artist's Professional League presented her with an award for the same naturalistic pheasants.

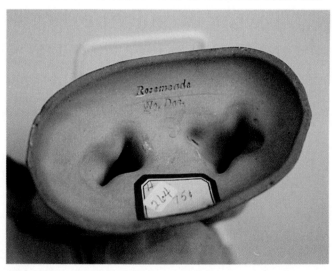

Extremely rare bisque red clay donkey carrier with saddlebags hanging from each side and cactus underneath, 4¼" x 5". More than one of these donkeys was made as a damaged one recently sold at auction. Mark on bottom of donkey carrier shown on right.

In 1951, Laura Taylor Hughes attained national recognition from the American Artists Professional League, the Citation Award for "meritorious and distinguished service in the field of ceramics." She received their State of North Dakota award in 1952.

The company name was changed from Wahpeton Pottery Company to Rosemeade Potteries in 1953. Robert Hughes announced the new name in a February 2, 1953 local newspaper article. "We found it too confusing for our distant patrons and salesmen to remember two names so we decided to concentrate on the name of our product."[70]

Previous company promotions listed "Wahpeton Pottery Co., Manufacturer of Rosemeade Pottery." With its connection to the state flower and a county township, this tradename also provided good company name recognition for state residents.

Howard Lewis served as production manager for twelve years during the heyday of the Wahpeton Pottery Company. However by 1956, with production slowing down, Lewis felt "we couldn't keep going with three partners"[71] and sold his shares to the Hughes.

Howard Lewis taught engineering, geology, and mathematics at the North Dakota State College of Science, Wahpeton, until 1973. He retired in Wahpeton and died in 1993.

When Howard Lewis left the company in 1956, Joe McLaughlin, who had previously worked for Red Wing Potteries, Red Wing, Minnesota, as assistant ceramic engineer and company foreman, was hired as production manager. McLaughlin, ceramic engineering graduate of Ohio State University with experience as plant manager at Hyalyn Porcelain, Hickory, North Carolina, brought new concepts to Rosemeade. Joe McLaughlin reintroduced white clay usage, started decal decoration, and accelerated advertising specialties sales.

Joe McLaughlin stated that during his years at Rosemeade Potteries there were only two salesmen, at most. Rosemeade was usually only a side line for a salesman. Joe and Betty McLaughlin themselves had booths at several three-day trade shows in cities like Fargo, North Dakota; Kansas City, Missouri; and Fort Dodge, Iowa.

After Laura Taylor Hughes died from cancer in 1959 at age 56, Joe McLaughlin continued the work of Rosemeade Potteries with the help of nine employees. Joe did the designing, mainly vases and specialty items. "Nothing along the line of figurines,"[72] he stated. The

Joe McLaughlin, production manager

majority of Rosemeade pottery was still made from North Dakota sandy clay, but white clay was also used until the company closed.

Joe McLaughlin reminisced, "The pottery industry itself was fascinating because things never seemed set. Firing conditions would change. Clay mixtures needed adjusting and glazes needed to be developed. It was very satisfying to start something new and see it become beautiful and salable."[73]

Already in 1953, "Copies of Rosemeade pieces, many of them quite crude, pop up now and then on gift ware counters." At that time, Laura Hughes said, "We don't worry about them. Perhaps some day I'll start a collection of copies."[74] However, in 1954, Howard Lewis saw "business slowing down."[75] Joe McLaughlin stated that by 1957, "Sales and demand for Rosemeade had declined due to cheap Japanese imports. For example, we found items for sale in stores that were copies of our wares. They were evidently made in molds from our pieces because they were smaller due to firing shrinkage. They were being retailed at prices less than our wholesale prices."[76]

Stacks of delinquent payment notices indicating accounts turned over for collection to the Dunn and Bradstreet Mercantile Claims Division, Minneapolis, show difficulty obtaining payment for products shipped. Retailer bankruptcy notices also appear in company files.

After World War II, Japan with its widely available clay, low wages, and time-honored technology streamlined its ceramic industry and vastly accelerated production. Without tariffs or import quotas, the United States became a ready market. Many of America's own potteries were driven out of business by these inexpensive Japanese ceramics. Laura Taylor Hughes' death and a new state minimum wage law also contributed to the company ending production in 1961.

After Rosemeade Potteries closed, Joe McLaughlin also taught at the North Dakota State College of Science, Wahpeton. McLaughlin was a faculty member in the architectural department for twenty years before retiring and moving to Arizona.

Betty McLaughlin, Rosemeade's last employee

Betty McLaughlin became the last Rosemeade employee. Known as "Mrs. Mac," Betty stayed on after the pottery closed to help Robert Hughes. Betty described "huge bins"[77] of salt and pepper shakers left in inventory. Besides sales to individuals, thousands of salt and peppers in a variety of subjects were sold to "a carnival man" for ten cents a pair, according to

Betty McLaughlin. These Rosemeade products became carnival prizes at fairs and midways around the country. In 1964, the remaining Rosemeade pottery and paper stickers were sent to the Richland County Historical Museum, which continued to sell this stock in the 1990s.

Laura Taylor Hughes praised her husband, Robert, as her greatest supporter. "He had faith enough in my ability as a designer and potter to go into the business with me, and help me carry out my plans which I had made so long before."[78] The son of a Welsh immigrant who started a Wahpeton bicycle shop, Hughes bought the local newspaper and printing plant. He later served as President of the Wahpeton National Bank from 1926 – 1953. Robert Hughes received numerous honors, including 1951 Rotary Outstanding Community Service, 1962 Wahpeton Chamber of Commerce Citizen of the Year, 1962 North Dakota State School of Science Alumnus of the Year, and the 1976 Red River Historical Society Home Fame Award.

"Mr. Wahpeton" was a major community benefactor. By the time he died at age ninety-six, Robert Hughes had left everything to the people through philanthropic contributions of Chahinkapa Park, the 18-hole Bois De Sioux Golf Course, and the Richland County Historical Museum. "Robert Hughes had the gift of foresight, with an attitude of optimism toward the possibilities of the immediate area....His mission to provide something of permanent value for the people of the community was a success."[79]

The Richland County Historical Museum became the Hughes' legacy. Already in 1946, Robert and Laura Hughes met with local residents to discuss forming a county historical society to keep alive the early history of pioneers. Laura Hughes kept the dream of a museum alive, and during her long illness, made plans to will money for its building. After Laura's death, Robert Hughes became a major benefactor of the museum which opened July 1, 1965. The museum displays a major Rosemeade pottery collection (Appendix II).

PROCESS/SWIRL

The Wahpeton Pottery Company and later Rosemeade Potteries used various methods for pottery making. Laura Taylor listed them as throwing, casting, jiggering, and pressing.[1]

Some early Rosemeade pottery was thrown on the potter's wheel, "The most artistic and poetic means of fashioning clay where every shape necessarily differs in feature and form from the preceding ones."[2] An ancient method, the wheel was in common use in Egypt's Valley of the Nile at least 4,000 years ago. The potter's wheel is a flat round disc supported on an upright pivot and turned about in a horizontal plane, like a record on a phonograph. As the name describes, the clay is thrown outwards by the force of the rotating wheel.

Throwing a pot on the wheel.

Although the majority of Rosemeade was molded, Laura Taylor described throwing as a process she used in her pottery making at the company.[3] An early company brochure stated, "Much of the Rosemeade ware is fashioned on the potter's wheel. This ancient method, known as 'throwing' gives each hand-made piece a charm and individuality of its own."[4] A 1940 article mentioned that "several experienced potters (were) employed as a new industry is established."[5]

Tony Lanz and his cousin Frank Lantz made hand-thrown ware for the Wahpeton Pottery Company. A photograph in the Richland County Museum archives shows Frank throwing a vase on the potter's wheel and Rosemeade pieces display his signature.

A company stock listing sheet and early company booklet (page 185) included the following "Hand-Thrown Glazed Ware:" vases in assorted shapes, bud vases, candleholders, bowls, flower baskets, pitchers, cream and sugar sets, and hats. Prices ranged from fifty cents to $2.50. "Hand-Thrown Badlands Ware" was also listed and priced. During the war, Laura Taylor stated that, "We stored our potters wheel and changed over entirely to casting our pottery."[6] Laura Taylor's March 25, 1943 letter to the well-known Wall Drug Store in Wall, South Dakota, emphasized the problem. "Due to the difficulty of getting skilled help to operate the potter's wheel we have had to discontinue for the time being the making of pitchers, cream and sugar sets and Badlands ware."[7]

After Howard Lewis came to the company in 1944, he started making swirl ware. Lewis stated that he also made other hand-thrown vases and bowls besides the swirl ware for a short time. Lewis was skilled at the wheel, having previous experience at several other potteries.

The majority of Rosemeade was cast in plastic molds, "a quick, accurate, reliable process where each pot made in same the mold is exactly like its brother."[8] Because of its time-saving value, the casting method was used constantly in commercial production.

Margaret Cable described the following process used at UND to make cast pottery. Laura Taylor Hughes later used the same techniques with Rosemeade. First, a solid model, the original object, is created, either formed by hand from modeling clay or hand-thrown on the wheel. The model, "a three-dimensional object made or used as a prototype or pattern, is used to create a mold from which a series of identical reproductions can eventually be made."[9]

Hand-built prototype of monkey figurine, used to create a mold. Occasionally, the collector may find a figure which has been modeled or shaped free hand. Prototype hand-built items were used as the original objects in making molds or were made to experiment with form and color.

Plaster of Paris, a white powder mixed with water, forms a thick creamy liquid which is poured over the solid model. The plaster hardens into a porous, absorbent state. The mold, called a block mold, is opened so that the solid model can be withdrawn. The block mold is reassembled and a plaster duplicate of the original, called a case mold, is made by filling the hollow with liquid plaster of Paris.

"The final or working model is made by casting plaster of Paris around the case mold and then removing the working mold after the plaster has set."[10] Commercial ware pieces are formed in this working mold.

The empty plaster mold is now filled with liquid clay called slip. As the pores of the plaster begin to absorb water from the liquid, the clay is drawn to the sides of the mold, where it forms a clay layer or cast. The thickness of the wall depends upon the length of time the clay remains in the mold. When the walls of the clay cast are the desired thickness, the excess liquid clay is drained out. The hollow cast of soft, wet clay left inside is the exact size and shape as the interior of the plaster mold. After further drying and hardening in the mold, the mold is opened and the casting removed.

The cast pieces, called greenware, go next to the finishers. First, the finishers wash and clean the greenware. Next, they trim and sponge edges and seams, in preparation for the first firing.

After the first firing, the ware, called bisque ware, is hand-painted by women decorators, using artist brushes. According to former employees, one decora-

LEFT:
Plaster duplicate of the original mountain goat prototype, produced as part of the mold making process, with experimental clear plastic horns.

RIGHT:
Standard Rosemeade mountain goat on left compared with hollow plaster mold figurine on right.

Mold of ducks with greenware duck.

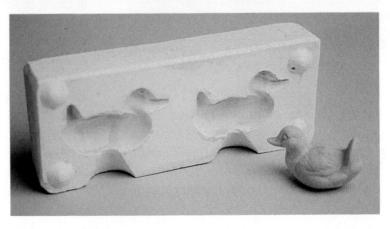

tor would paint the whole piece. Former decorators also stated that no quotas were set, and they worked at their own pace.

Although most Rosemeade ware was molded, decorative handwork made each different. Because of this hand painting, "Most of the work is handwork....This gives each cup and figure a little individuality of its own,"[11] according to Laura Taylor.

Following a second firing, orders were packed into boxes with newspaper filler. Most orders were filled by mail. A former employee stated that an entire day's production would be packed into Howard Lewis' car to be taken to the post office. Joe McLaughlin related that he also made post office runs with his station wagon. Some orders were taken to the local depot and shipped by railroad.

Warren Olson and Leo Paulson casting molds.

Finishers at work, Ella Johnson, Emma Althoff, and Signe Bjerkager.

Bisque ware, following the first firing.

Decorators Cora Olson, Rose Ann Puetz, Blanch Conlon, Betty Jane Wateland, and Louise Keeney.

Josephine Murray and Olga Hektner packing orders.

Jiggering, "a mechanical method of making repetition shapes on the wheel with plaster molds and profiles,"[12] was also a Rosemeade method. The jigger is a power-driven revolving turntable used with a profile, which is an outline of a vessel's body. A mold may be used to produce pots on a large scale without the time necessary with hand throwing. Documentation shows that Laura Taylor used this method at UND.

Laura Taylor mentioned pressing as a method used at Rosemeade. Another way to shape ceramic products, soft clay is pushed or pressed by hand into the mold crevices until the entire inner surface is covered. Plaster molds or molds of other materials are used "to obtain an impression of even the most minute details"[13] for three-dimensional or flat pieces. After the clay shrinks slightly, the object can be removed from the mold.

Malleable rubber cavity used as mold.

Most clay for the pottery came from a deposit four miles west of Mandan, North Dakota. This clay was part of the Slope Formation, dating to about sixty million years ago. Laura Taylor found the clay "particularly suitable for pottery making."[14] In 1952, the Wahpeton

Piles of clay weathering behind the company building.

Pottery Company was paying $14.71 for a ton of clay from Marcus Gress, Mandan.

Howard Lewis did not agree with Laura Taylor regarding the clay quality. Lewis described the clay as "not very good pottery clay, hard to work with." He cited the conclusion in a report from a chemical company, "This clay can't be made into pottery." Chemicals added to the clay to produce faster drying in the molds were ineffective. The molds could only be used once a day and had to dry under heat bulbs between castings.

Clay was left piled up behind the plant for up to a year. "The longer it weathers in the sun and rain the better it seems to be."[15] Without such weathering, the clay would stick in the molds. "The only preparation necessary in preparing the clay is to soak it in water and strain it through a fine sieve, whereas most pottery clays must be mixed with other clays or materials,"[16] according to Laura Taylor.

Red clay was used in the early 1940s for a limited number of products, including a bear, horse, and kangaroo. According to a former employee, the red clay was not suitable for matt glazes. The reddish color would show through the glaze and, with aging, get darker.[17]

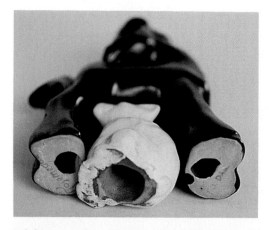

Red clay was used to make the Rosemeade black horse and white bear.

Sandy clay kangaroo on left and red clay kangaroos on right, all Rosemeade products.

Laura Taylor used some white clay during the early years of Wahpeton Pottery Company production. Early white clay examples include the bisque penguin, geographical center obelisk, and Indian God of Peace, all made before the Joe McLaughlin era, according to McLaughlin. An article on file at the Richland County Historical Museum describes two figurines of the Indian God of Peace as being of different size and color, one made from white clay and the other from North Dakota clay. "Taylor used a clay she bought from Kentucky. Though the clay shrunk less and produced a whiter final product, customers objected and she returned to the exclusive use of North Dakota clay."[18]

The extremely rare penguin is not only an early piece made of white clay but also bisque ware.

Rosemeade bisque pieces are scarce, being made early in the pottery's production in limited quantities. Bisque ware has been fired but not glazed. With unglazed ware, the decorations, either incised or impressed, and the modeling are more prominent as glazes obscure the details. Some hand painting was applied to the Rosemeade bisque ware.

In the late 1950s, Joe McLaughlin turned to widespread use of white clay shipped from Kentucky. McLaughlin stated that they started using white clay after he conferred with Robert Hughes. Mr. Hughes felt that they had saturated the area with their pottery, which was not selling as well as previously. Because of decreased sales, Hughes had been susidizing the pottery from his own money for two to three years, and their sales force had diminished to one salesman.

McLaughlin found molding pottery with North Dakota clay difficult. Molds could only be used once daily because adding the large quantities of necessary water to the clay slowed drying. With the white clay drying faster, the molds could be used two or three times a day in a more cost effective manner. White clay also shrunk less than the North Dakota clay, producing a whiter final product which was more suitable for decals.

Under Joe McLaughlin's direction, Rosemeade Pottery started using decorative decals during the last three years of production, 1958 – 1961. Lithography, known as decalcomania in the United States, was already being used on East Liverpool, Ohio, tableware produced during the 1890s. In 1918, Margaret Cable wrote to several companies seeking "decalcomania patterns in conventional designs suitable for use on a cream colored body"[19] at the University of North Dakota.

"Decals provided potters with the means for making colorful decorations in one step,"[20] with one firing, thus lowering decorating costs. Also, highly skilled painters were no longer necessary as less experience and skill were required to apply the decals. A 1965 *Popular Ceramics* issue stated that "competition with foreign markets with inexpensive labor"[21] established a trend back toward decal usage in the 1950s and 1960s.

All decals were custom made for Rosemeade by a Fort Smith, Arkansas, lithography printing firm. Joe McLaughlin sent the design, which was printed onto special paper using a silk screening process and then covered with a plastic medium. Because the decal manufacturer chosen by McLaughlin was expert in ceramic colors and chromolithographic printing, the prints were high quality but more expensive than most others.

Joe McLaughlin described the process used in making a Rosemeade decal-decorated item, for example, an ashtray. The ashtray was first cast from white clay and the greenware allowed to dry. Then, the first firing made it bisque ware. The bisque piece was sprayed with a clear glaze and fired the second time to mature the glaze. Next, the decal was applied by soaking the pattern off the paper and sponging and squeezing it onto the ware. "During the third firing, the plastic medium burned away, leaving the fully fired color decoration."[22] This firing "matured" the decal so that the decal would sink into the glaze. The decal could not be scratched or worn off later.

Glazed white tiles, round and square, were purchased and not made by Rosemeade, according to McLaughlin. After these tiles were purchased, the decals were applied at Rosemeade and then fired to mature the decals. "We could buy the tiles cheaper than we could make them." [23] These tiles were sold as both trivets and wall plaques.

Some tiles may be found with a Wheeling Tile Company mark. This Wheeling, West Virginia, tile company made vitreous, nonporous tile until about 1960 and appears to have sold undecorated tile to various pottery companies. [24]

Wooden frames were also purchased. The decals were applied to the tiles which were then mounted at Rosemeade and sold to the public. McLaughlin described the basswood, light-colored wooden frames as hand-turned in a northern Minnesota garage and mailed to the pottery. The round wooden frames in walnut or maple were purchased from North Carolina and not hand-turned.

There has been a question over the years regarding whether wooden framed trivets were given to Rosemeade employees as Christmas gifts. According to Joe McLaughlin, "We couldn't afford to give them away." [25] Former Rosemeade employees also did not remember such gifts.

Plates were not made at Rosemeade. Again, the plates were purchased from another company, decals were applied and then fired.

White ashtrays were made from white clay at Rosemeade Pottery. Several pottery companies of the time made similar white ashtrays. Joe McLaughlin related that a gold band was usually applied around the center of Rosemeade white ashtrays. Examples include Dakota Territory Centennial memorabilia.

Wheeling Tile Company tile fired with a Les Kouba pheasant decal and sold as a Rosemeade trivet.

Emma Althoff, former employee who painted gold bands on the ashtrays, described the process. The bands were applied to glazed ware using a liquid form of 24K gold. With her elbow resting at a proper height, she would angle her loaded brush to paint inside the tray, while her other hand rotated the ashtray on a turntable. The ashtray was fired to make the gold band permanent. At the end of the working day, the brushes were soaked overnight in solvent. Because the gold would not adhere unless the brush was completely clean, Emma told of "tasting the brush to see if it was clean enough." [26]

Glazes provide pottery with its luscious brilliance, subtle tones, and varied range of colors. "A change in

Miniature pitchers used to test and show glaze colors.

Glaze testers — "ROSEMEADE POTTERY" on front, numbers and initials incised on bottom or with black pen; 52 colors have been seen.

glaze or color can affect the overall image of a piece,"[27] often determining aesthetic appeal and rarity.

During firing, the melting glaze coating becomes glass, fusing into the body of the ware. This glassy finish serves dual purposes. First, the glaze adds a waterproof coating, making the vessel impervious to water. Secondly, the glaze enhances the vessel's appearance, "transforming dull clay into a thing of living beauty."[28]

Most Rosemeade pottery underwent two firings. The first or bisque firing at around 1,600°F hardened the clay into permanent forms and made it absorbent to glaze. After glaze was applied, the ware was then given a second firing at around 2,050°F.

Clifford Dahm at the kiln, firing Rosemeade pottery.

In discussing the company's source of glaze material, Laura Taylor noted, "We use some of the same clay in the glaze from which the ware is made. The other materials come from South Dakota, where it is mined and processed, and mineral oxides from pottery supply houses."[29]

During the early years, Laura Taylor experimented with glazes, applying her University of North Dakota knowledge. Taylor indicated that glazes were a major problem. "Commercial glazes can be bought but they are expensive and often unsatisfactory. If a glaze has not been worked out especially for the clay on which it is to be used, it will often craze or crack."[30]

By December 1940, months of Taylor's experimentation resulted in several new glazes. These included Meadow Green, Dusty Rose, and Mirror Blue.

The new colors were "suitable for characteristic North Dakota designs."[31] A Rosemeade advertising brochure described Harvest Gold as "a blending of amber

Rare Harvest Gold glaze 7" vase with motif of three running horses, $350.00+.

and red which when fired at different temperatures, provides effects as varied and unexpected as a ripening field of grain or autumn leaves after frost."[32]

After Howard Lewis joined the company, he took over glaze experimentation and production. Because Lewis continued to concoct glazes to fit the specific clay properties, instead of using commercial glazes, most crazing was eliminated. Crazing (small cracks appearing in the clay body) occurs when the glaze pulls away as the glaze shrinks more than the clay during firing. According to Lewis, the pottery would shrink up to ten percent.

The metallic bronze glaze was brought from Broadmoor Pottery, Denver, Colorado, according to Howard Lewis, who worked there from 1938 to 1939. Lewis related that while he was trying unsuccessfully to create the bronze glaze at Broadmoor, another employee "said 'try this' and handed me a slip of paper with the bronze glaze formula."[33]

The vivid colorful Rosemeade pottery hues are the most distinctive. These unique lustrous glazes set Rosemeade apart, making it easily recognizable. Metal oxides painted under the glazes "became partially absorbed in the glaze and run slightly in firing, creating a true ceramic effect."[34] Marion Nelson, nationally recognized art pottery historian, further described the buff-colored clay body as showing "through enough to bring the applied colors into harmony. The whites are painted with slips, which stand out as bright accents on the blended grounds." Laura Taylor stated in a 1950 letter, "The semi-transparent glazes which we use help to bring out the carefully modeled detail."[35]

Glazes were applied to Rosemeade wares by different methods. Dip glazing, plunging the vessel into a large container of liquid glaze, is the simplest method but uses more glaze.

Poured glazes, with the glaze poured over the vessel, use less glaze. Poured glazes can be applied to a variety of shapes, for example, just the inside of a vessel.

Sprayed glazes are applied with an atomizer, called an airbrush, a procedure developed by Laura Fry at Rookwood Pottery. An electric spray gun was used for Rosemeade pottery. Timed bursts of spray are directed at a revolving pot. For a two-toned effect, the piece is first sprayed with a base coat and then lightly sprayed with a contrasting color. Although there is more waste, this method "permits the most delicate shading and blending of color."[36] Laura Taylor learned this method at UND where the "soft blended and shaded effects characterize this pottery."[37]

Rare hand-thrown 3½" vase, shaded bluish to pink, glaze applied with atomizer, "NORTH DAKOTA Rosemeade" mark, $250.00+.

Hand-brushing the glaze onto the vessel is more time intensive and, therefore, more costly. For example, Laura Taylor stated that she had to set the Paul Bunyan and Blue Ox salt and pepper pair at a higher price because of "spending so much time on the decorating."[38]

Rare early pieces of Rosemeade were decorated with drip glazing. The piece is covered with a base glaze. Then a very soft second glaze is applied to the

edge of the piece. The second glaze moves during firing, dripping down over the base glaze.

Three extremely rare hand-thrown drip glaze bowls.

During earlier years, holes in the ashtray matched holes in the figurine base. Gluing through the holes applied the figurine to the ashtray.

During Joe McLaughlin's era, holes were not used. After the ashtray was glazed, the figurine was set upon the ashtray. During firing, the heat would fuse the figurine onto the ashtray.

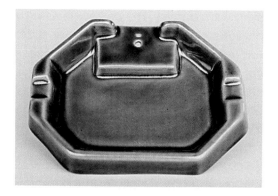

Ashtray with hole for gluing figurine.

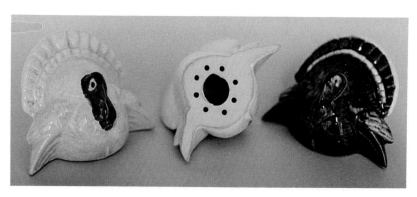

Turkey figurines with holes used for gluing onto snack trays.

Swirl ware was produced in the early years of the Wahpeton Pottery Company. Laura Taylor may have learned to make swirl pottery during her time at the Dickinson Clay Products Company in 1937. The Dickinson company was known for their "Dickota Badlands" swirl ware. Swirl pottery was also made by the North Dakota WPA while Laura Taylor was project supervisor. One of the WPA potters, Frank Lantz, is known to have worked for the Wahpeton Pottery Company in the early 1940s.

An early company stock listing sheet and company booklet (page 185) offered "Hand-thrown Bad Lands Ware." Vases, bowls, pitchers, cream and sugar sets, ashtrays, and hats were priced from fifty cents to $1.50. In 1943, a letter from Laura Taylor stated that Badlands ware "would be discontinued for the time being." [39]

When Howard Lewis came to the Wahpeton Pottery Company in 1944, he was proficient at making swirl pottery. His "Dickota Badlands" was Dickinson Clay Prod-

RIGHT:
Rare 2½" x 2¾" swirl vase, marked "Rosemeade BADLANDS," $500.00+. The crumpled rim of this early swirl vase is uncharacteristic of later Rosemeade swirl ware. This rim resembles George Ohr pottery made in Biloxi, Mississippi, which was famous for its crushed, twisted, and folded shapes.

LEFT:
"Rosemeade BADLANDS" black ink stamp mark.

RIGHT:
Rare 4⅜" x 3" swirl horse, marked "BADLANDS," $500.00+. Colored clay for the horse was pressed into a mold, with the eyes incised later by hand.

LEFT:
"BADLANDS" black ink stamp mark. Early swirl pieces appear to have been marked "Rosemeade BADLANDS" or just "BADLANDS."

ucts Company's best-known pottery. Howard Lewis was soon hand throwing swirl vases and pitchers at the Wahpeton Pottery Company. Lewis stated that the swirl ware was made in limited quantity for a short time. He added that these swirl pieces were sold at the pottery, never through salesmen.

Swirl ware resembles North Dakota's southwestern landscape. Steep canyons, towering spires, and rugged hills created a colorful painted landscape of haunting shapes and shades, the Badlands. Red, blue, green, brown, gray, and creamy-white clays, reminiscent of the subtle landscape coloration, are swirled together on the potter's wheel to create swirl pottery.

Howard Lewis learned the swirl process by watching Charles D. Hyten, creative owner of Niloak Pottery, Benton, Arkansas. However, Lewis stated repeatedly that he worked mainly with the Hywood line at Niloak and did not make swirl ware while there.

To make swirl ware pottery, the potter starts with white clay and adds oxides — cobalt blue for blue, ferric oxide for red, chromic oxide for gray, copper oxide for green, iron oxide for brown, and tin oxide for white. The potter then pulls slabs of the colored clay together, cuts the layers, and throws the mixture on the wheel. Stripes are formed as the pottery is pulled up. Mixing clays for swirl is a difficult procedure as the various colored clays tend to shrink and separate after firing. "Colors must also be carefully planned in relationship to each other for harmony and appearance."[40]

Because it is sometimes difficult to distinguish unmarked Rosemeade ware from unmarked Dickota Badlands pottery, all pieces pictured are marked Rosemeade on the bottom. All pictured swirl pieces have a matt glaze exterior and glossy glaze interior, unless noted otherwise.

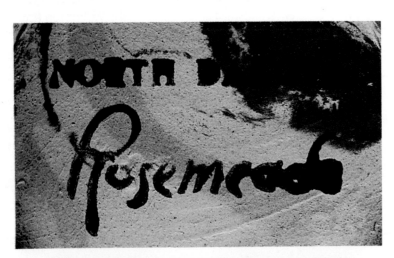

"NORTH DAKOTA Rosemeade" black ink stamp mark of later swirl ware.

Swirl cloverleaf bowl, 1½" x 3½", $200.00+.

Vases with glossy glaze inside and outside, 4¾" brown/tan vase and 3¾" blue/tan vase, $250.00+ each.

Two-color 4¾" vase, $200.00+.

Two-color 3¼" pitcher, $200.00+.

Three-color 3¾" vase, $200.00+.

The tan solid-color handle was applied after the piece was hand-thrown. Handles on Rosemeade swirl pieces tend to be solid colored instead of swirled.

Two three-color vases, 4¾" and 5¼", $200.00+ each.

Two-color 3" pitcher, $200.00+.

2" x 3¼" three-color, unusual-shaped pitcher with pinched handle, $200.00+.

Swirl ware: two-color 4" vase with top and bottom rims, three-color 3¼" pitcher, two-color 3" vase, three-color 2¾" pitcher, three-color 3¾" vase, $200.00+ each.

Three-color swirl: 2½" x 2⅜" vase; pinched handle 2¾" x 3½" pitcher; 2½" x 2" vase, $200.00+ each.

Flared top, three-colored 4⅛" vase, 3¾" green/creme vase with glossy glaze exterior, 3½" two-colored pitcher, $200.00+ each.

Three-color swirl: 5" vase; 6¼" vase, 5½" vase, $200.00+ each.

Three-color swirl 5" vase with large 4¼" opening, $200.00+.

Three-color swirl 3" pitcher with 3½" wide mouth, $200.00+.

Glossy glaze exterior and interior two-color 3⅛" vase, $250.00+.

Two-color 3" swirl vase, $200.00+.

Four-color 8¼" swirl vase with unglazed interior, $300.00+.

Three-color 8" swirl vase with unglazed interior, $300.00+.

PROCESS/SWIRL

Some Rosemeade pieces were painted to resemble swirl clay. This effect may have been achieved by use of a sponge or brush. The intermingled colors appear only on the surface and not throughout the pot. These pieces are called marbelized, giving the surface appearance of marble, instead of swirl.

Extremely rare 3" pitcher with blue gloss glaze interior and blue, tan, brown painted swirl.

Extremely rare 6¾" x 6½" piece with holes, unglazed interior and blue, reddish brown, tan painted swirl, intended function is unknown, perhaps lamp base. This piece is unmarked but a plaster prototype from the Laura Taylor Hughes collection is on display at the Richland County Historical Museum.

Extremely rare painted marbelized effect 4¼" Geographical Center figurine.

COLLECTING

Much Rosemeade pottery is marked with an impressed mark or an ink stamp of the company name in black or blue lettering on the bottom. Many of the marks are shown and described here. However, other variations may exist. No record of all marks used or years of usage has been found. Employees thought they were making inexpensive things of little value. At the time, they did not recognize the quality of the glaze. They did not realize that the prairie motifs coupled with other indigenous North Dakota pottery characteristics would reflect the culture of that era. Therefore, items were not systematically stamped. Precise records were not kept. Today, many questions arise due to this.

Ink stamp mark, used most frequently, in black or blue.

Ink stamp mark.

Ink stamp mark.

Ink stamp mark.

Ink stamp mark.

"N. D." ink stamp mark.

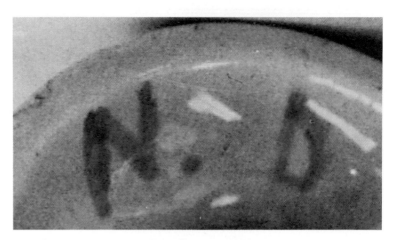

Handwritten "N. D." mark.

Hand-incised "Rosemeade N. D." mark on bottom of early horse pitcher.

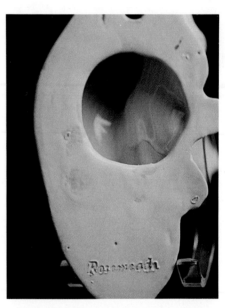

Mark impressed into mold.

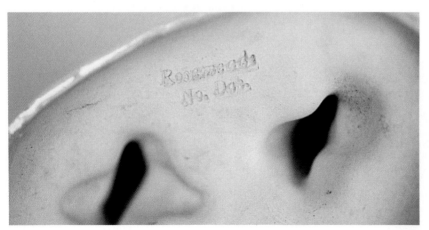

Mark impressed into mold; "No. Dak." sometimes appears above the "Rosemeade."

Foil paper stickers showing the prairie rose and "Rosemeade NO. DAK." were used frequently. Since these stickers were often lost or removed, many Rosemeade pieces are unmarked. The stickers are shown in the order it appears they were used chronologically. However, employees indicated that whatever stickers happened to be available were applied. Therefore, the stickers are sometimes inaccurate for dating pieces.

Determining whether a specific piece was made in the early or late years of Rosemeade pottery production would be possible by using research and employee information or studying company products and marks. For example, early hand-thrown pieces are usually marked "NORTH DAKOTA Rosemeade," "No. Dak. Rosemeade," or "N. D. Rosemeade." Joe McLaughlin addressed this question of dating pieces by stickers or marks as "very difficult." McLaughlin added that all Rosemeade was not uniformly marked like Rookwood pottery.

Dating of all marks and pieces has not been considered necessary. The company was only in production for a twenty-one year span, during an era considered modern or contemporary.

According to Joe McLaughlin, leftover Rosemeade Kouba decals were sent to Les Kouba in Minneapolis after the company closed. The decals were applied to objects like wall plaques and ashtrays (page 78). Some of these decals were recently sold at the Kouba estate sale. Although the decals are Rosemeade memorabilia items, there should be no concern regarding possible use on pottery items because of the brittle aged condition of the decals and the process necessary for application to pottery.

The paper Rosemeade stickers pose a different problem because they are easily applied. For years, people brought items they considered to be Rosemeade to the Richland County Historical Museum, where paper stickers were applied. Many questions have arisen

Silver prairie roses with four petals and leaves pointed out to side.

Pale pink prairie roses with four petals and leaves pointed out to side.

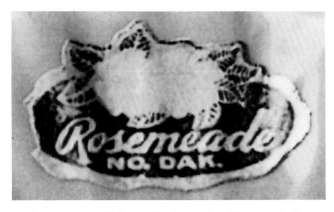

Peach prairie roses with five overlapping petals and leaves projecting out at top of sticker.

Bright pink prairie roses with five overlapping petals and leaves projecting out at top of sticker.

Les Kouba "Walleyed Pike" decals.

Pheasant salt and pepper shakers with sticker, "Souvenir of BEACH, NO. DAKOTA."

regarding the identity of some items with paper Rosemeade stickers.

When sold as souvenirs, pieces may display other stickers. These stickers were added by the promoting business, town, state, or park, and not by Rosemeade Potteries.

An ink stamp or incised mark of the promoting enterprise was applied on some pieces. Often no Rosemeade stamp appears on these pieces.

A mark identifying artist Anne Krzyzaniak, by initials or name, appears on some Rosemeade pottery, particularly lapel pins. According to early employee Olga Hektner, Anne was a friend of Laura Taylor. A card table was set up for her whenever she wished to come into the factory and hand paint pieces.

Potter Frank Lantz created hand-thrown Rosemeade pottery during the early years. Some of his pieces are signed.

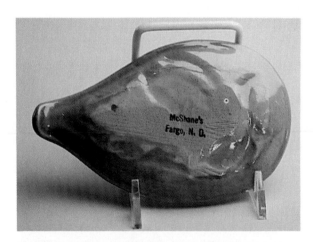

Flying pheasant tray with black ink stamp,"McShane's Fargo, N. D."

Prairie rose plate with blue ink stamp, "MINOT, N. D."

Incised "Chahinkapa No. Dak." mark on teepee ashtray made for sale at the Chahinkapa Park, Wahpeton.

Les Kouba pheasant decal mug with black ink stamp, "HAUSAUER."

The initials "AK" on a heart-shaped pin.

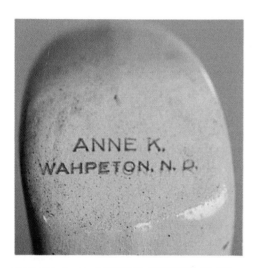

The bottom of the Norwegian girl was marked with Anne's "AK" initials and black ink stamp "ANNE K. WAHPETON, N. D."

Black ink stamp of "ANNE K. WAHPETON, N. D." on bottom of shoe.

Incised signature "F. Lantz" on bottom of hand-thrown bowl.

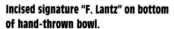

At first, imperfect pieces were thrown into a wheelbarrow and destroyed after quality inspection by Laura Taylor. However, "Many pieces were salvaged by employees so a decision was made to sell the 'imperfects' or 'seconds.'"[1] Pieces were considered seconds because of defects like pin holes, misshapen forms, and poor coloring. Newspaper ads of the time advertised discontinued items and seconds "priced below cost of manufacture" with "most half of retail price."[2] Although dealers occasionally asked to sell seconds, all such requests were denied. "As always, no imperfect pieces of Rosemeade pottery or seconds are sold to dealers. All such pieces have always been sold at the factory salesroom."[3]

Ink stamp "SECOND" mark.

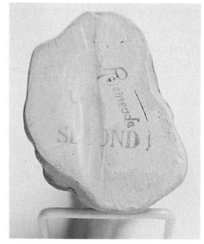

Some cast pieces were deliberately made to look handmade. According to a local newspaper, Laura Taylor would shape the prototype bowl or vase on the potter's wheel. Then a mold was cast of the slightly irregular model "to retain much of the quaint irregularity of hand-thrown work."[4] Joe McLaughlin also described these pieces. Cast pieces made to look handmade only have the irregular ridges on the outside. With a hand-thrown piece made on the wheel, the ridges made by the potter's hand can be observed and felt on the inside of the pot.

Vase made to look handmade, smooth on interior and with irregular ridges on exterior.

Occasionally, Rosemeade shapes are discovered with much different painting than factory produced items. Groups like the Boy Scouts and Girl Scouts toured the pottery. Sometimes members were allowed to paint bisque ware. The pieces were then fired for them, and they returned to receive the finished items. With other groups, bisque ware was taken home to be painted by members and not refired. Former employees tell of bringing home bisque ware and of others coming to the plant for it. After the company closed,

Ducks painted by Boy Scouts and not fired the second time, according to former employees.

Rosemeade molds were taken to the dump by the truckload. Some townspeople went out to the dump and retrieved molds. Two bushel baskets of bisque ware sold at a Wahpeton auction a few years ago. Therefore, Rosemeade shapes surface with different glazes than those used on factory pieces.

Rosemeade pottery molds were sometimes sold to hobby shops. These became hobby molds as the molds were used to make ceramic greenware painted in classes or homes as a hobby. Greenware is ware taken directly from molds to be decorated before any firing.

Berg Ceramics, Wahpeton, bought molds from Rosemeade Potteries and made greenware from these molds. The greenware from Rosemeade molds was then used in the Berg ceramics classes or wholesaled to other shops. Delores Berg, owner, stated that these molds included sugar and creamer sets, lunch sets, vases, and Minnesota and North Dakota ashtrays.

According to Delores Berg, Berg Ceramics did not use pieces already fired and glazed at Rosemeade Potteries. The purchased molds were only used during Berg Ceramics' early years. The Rosemeade molds did not hold up well and greenware could be made more quickly in commercial molds.

Berg Ceramics pieces may be distinguished from Rosemeade products. Pieces made and decorated by Delores Berg were signed DAB. Students in the Berg classes scratched their names on the bottom of the greenware pieces. Berg Ceramics only used white clay.

Delores Berg of Berg Ceramics repaired broken Rosemeade pottery items. Berg called Rosemeade pottery "very difficult to repair. We did not have the paints to match the colors exactly."[5] it was also hard to get pieces to stick together so broken sections sometimes had to be drilled or cut with a saw tooth instrument.

Unmarked pieces can usually be recognized by the beach-sand color of the clay on the unglazed bases. Overall design features and glaze color are also important distinguishing characteristics. Japanese import copies of Rosemeade designs are usually easily recognizable. Decoration quality is poor. Colors are not true. The pottery copies are lighter in weight, while the solid plaster copies are too heavy. According to Joe McLaughlin, the Japanese imports were also one-tenth smaller in size.

Many Rosemeade products have cross-market or cross-over appeal and are sought by more than one group of collectors. These include banks, bells, televi-

The North Dakota 3" x 5¼" state map tray on the left was made from sandy clay and part of Rosemeade's product line. The tray on the right is bigger, 3¼" x 5¾", because it was made from white clay as a hobby mold and is not Rosemeade.

Different paint was used for the hobby mold tray, with "Danners Ceramics" scratched into the bottom.

The Rosemeade tray has holes at the top for hanging and the hobby mold does not.

sion lamps, jewelry, bookends, wall pockets, breweriana, salt and pepper shakers, and ashtrays.

This type of collecting is also considered generic collecting, "The acquisition of a specific class of item — with no thought or regard to the manufacturer."[6] Generic collecting can reflect an individual's personal tastes and provide endless choices without the drive to complete a collection.

Ashtrays, along with other tobacco-related products, have recently become popular with collectors. As the *Wall Street Journal* stated, "Some collectors have fond memories associated with cigarettes. Others appreciate the history that is told through tobacco products over the years. If you go back to when the Mayflower landed, this entire country's economy was built on the tobacco plant. There has never been any single product marketed more extensively."[7]

During the 1940s and 1950s, smoking was considered chic and glamorous, with possession of smoking accessories "another example of sophistication and good taste."[8] Rosemeade met the demand for utensils to facilitate smoking by producing vast quantities of

ashtrays. Many were three-dimensional advertisements promoting states, businesses, financial institutions, historical places, and products. Others appealed to the tourist market as souvenirs and novelties. Several forms were produced for use as both ashtrays and spoon rests.

Today, ashtrays "echo a vast industry — and way of life — forever changed by scientific inquiry into the effects of smoking upon our health."[9] "They (ashtrays) are seldom encountered now. To display a formal ashtray for use in the enlightened 1990's is to silently condone smoking, a questionable activity. Smoking is no longer in vogue."[10]

Jewelry collecting "has come to a new maturity... the ranks of those recognizing its value have blossomed many fold, raising prices tremendously."[11] Due to metal shortage, ceramic jewelry was given a popularity boost during World War II as a substitute for unavailable metallic jewelry. "Ceramic jewelry still has a place in the accessory field on account of the brilliance and sparkle of the glazes which are used on pottery clays."[12]

Ceramic pins, early Rosemeade company products, are scarce. Production was discontinued during the war. With the steel shortage, it was not possible to get metal pin fasteners for them. This fact may also account for the lack of fasteners on many of the available pins. An additional reason for the scarcity of ceramic pins is the high attrition rate, as ceramic jewelry is easily broken with usage.

"Still banks," **banks** with only coin slots and no moving parts, have been collected since colonial times with the hobby accelerating in America during the 1920s. Banks, collected as abstracts from real life, claim a long and venerable history. Ancient Roman and Greek excavations reveal examples up to 2,500 years old. The invention and saving of money are closely linked with banks. With the establishment of a coinage system and issuance of copper pennies in the 1790s, Americans began pursuing banks for savings. As William McKinley, twenty-fifth president of the United States, stated, "The little savings bank in the home means more for the future of a family, almost, than all the advice in the world. It gives them the right start."[13] The bank, often termed "piggy bank" because pigs were popular designs, became "a tiny family safe or an educational toy for children."[14] In earlier eras, banks were cherished by both adults and children as useful decorative objects or toys conveying thrift. Today, their widespread appeal continues for all ages.

Rosemeade banks, like many pottery banks, are available to collectors in limited numbers. Because there was no way to open these banks except to break them, few survived.

During the past decade, collector interest in **Western memorabilia**, including cowboy and Native American objects, has soared. Horace Greeley's admonition to "Go West, Young Man" has resurfaced as collectors "discover that the western United States...proves a veritable treasure trove of America."[15]

Attuned to current trends, the Wahpeton Pottery Company produced several versions of **television lamps.** During the early days of television, the prevailing widespread concern was eyesight damage caused by watching television in the dark. "The generation who grew up watching television between the late 1940s and early 1960s remembers with fondness their parents' stern admonition, 'You will go blind if you watch television in the dark.'"[16] Perceiving that direct lighting would affect picture quality, dim lighting was recommended by manufacturers. Thus, the birth of the "television lamp," invented to sit on the television and provide diffused light from a low wattage bulb at the back.

Between 1950 and 1960 the number of television sets owned by American families grew from three million to fifty million. With the television as the focal point of the living room, the television lamp became an attempt to decorate around the unbecoming "big glass eye." Many of these lamps "reflected the lingering influence of Art Deco design. Animal shapes were a popular choice, particularly the streamlined panther, symbolic of speed."[17] With indirect room lighting, the shapes appeared as silhouettes. Some shapes doubled as vases or planters, evidenced by Rosemeade's wolfhound.

"Virtually every U. S. citizen born since 1950 has been directly exposed to television, a unique characteristic which explains in large part the soaring interest in TV collectibles."[18] Collectors are turning to TV lamps which speak of 1950s popular culture.

Pottery **wall pockets** are also being discovered by collectors. Originally crafted to hold various household articles, wall pockets, sometimes called wall vases, are defined by collectors today as "flat–backed vases with a hole in the back for hanging."[19] Collectors enjoy wall pockets because they require only the limited display space of a wall. Most are in good condition, being rarely handled or used.

Wall pockets date back to the 1750s with Staffordshire potter Thomas Whildon's ware followed by other English potters like Spode and Wedgwood. With the Victorian era's emphasis on nature, wall pockets "evolved to fill a need for a wall-hung container to hold plants,"[20] like ivy. By the 1920s and 1930s, wall pockets had reached fad popularity in American homes.

Fredda Perkins, in her research of American potteries for *Wall Pockets of the Past,* "indicates that over 85 different companies at one time or other provided wall pockets in assorted styles."[21] The Wahpeton Pottery Company joined this circle of manufacturers, usually promoting these products as wall vases and sometimes using terms wall pockets and wall vases interchangeably.

Bookends, useful sculptures, continue to lure collectors. Matching sets function to accommodate books or provide a decorative accent for a room. Although first produced in England and Europe, "Nearly all the bookends ever made were made in this country. It is fair to say that bookends are a native American class of antiques, a contribution that we made to the world and an art form of which we can be proud."[22] Like other pottery companies, Rosemeade sometimes used the same designs as those of their other ceramic products, such as banks and figurines.

Perhaps some bookends were sold singly as doorstops. "A close relationship existed between doorstops and bookends."[23] Some companies even sold sets which included one doorstop and two bookends.

In the 1940s and 1950s, **flowerpots** were produced by many American pottery companies. During recent years, vintage flowerpots have become "sought after items to coordinate with the current garden decorating theme."[24] Some of these flowerpots are being used for their original purpose, filled with herbs and other house plants, while others are collected solely for their decorative interest. Condition is important as usage often caused cracks, chips, and lime deposits. Rosemeade flowerpots are not plentiful. Company stock lists indicated only a few variations and attrition is high on an item meant for constant use.

Candleholders have retained a special role throughout civilization. In early times, candles, one of the oldest forms of illumination, were essential. "When modern lighting fails, it is still our stand-by; no other light has the same dependability."[25] Many of today's candleholder collectors are also compelled by the romantic glow of flickering candlelight.

As an early twentieth century advertisement stated, "The lure of the **table lamp** is universal. You notice other people's lamps and they observe yours."[26] During that era, clean, effortless light was considered a miracle, and electricity not taken for granted. Today, an eye-appealing lamp is still an attention-getter. Wahpeton Pottery Company made horse motif lamps.

From the Old Testament book of Exodus to Egyptian tombs to the ruins of Ninevah, **bell** making has had an ancient history going back to about 3000 B.C. Throughout the centuries, the bell shape has changed little. The sphere, with small holes at its top and a slit on the bottom half, contains a tiny ball. When the bell is rung, the clapper swings from side to side, striking the inside of the bell. Besides their historic and cultural appeal, it is "the sound of bells that makes them come alive,"[27] for the myriad of bell collectors.

Breweriana refers to collectible items related to beer, brewery advertising and packaging. "Anything that mentions a beer brand is collectible,"[28] as the numbers of collectors grow. Several breweriana items were made by Rosemeade Potteries for liquor distributor, Hausauer Beverages.

During World War II, American potteries like the Wahpeton Pottery Company were able to grab the **salt and pepper shaker** market from the Japanese. "Shakers were wildly popular and manufacturing was at its peak during the 1940s and 1950s."[29] Nostalgia fueled a mid-1980s resurgence in interest in salt and pepper shaker collecting, which has continued.

Salt and pepper shakers are Rosemeade's most popular nationwide cross-over collectible, being eagerly sought by shaker collectors as well as by pottery collectors. Most of the shakers were also available as figurines, a practice commonly used by other potteries of the era, like the Ceramics Arts Studio.

Well known for quality, Mike Schneider, in *The Complete Salt and Pepper Shaker Book,* stated that Rosemeade "created and marketed some of the finest figural shakers that have ever been made."[30] "You would have to go a long way to beat the quality of Rosemeade's shakers, both naturalistic and stylized."[31]

Certain subjects are also cross-over collectibles, like dogs, cats, horses, and advertising. Some of these are discussed in the Product Lines chapter.

Rosemeade Potteries, a successful sales enterprise in its own time, responded to the needs and wishes of the public, expanding and introducing product lines. Today, Rosemeade pottery continues to be a popular collectible.

"As native to North Dakota as her state flower,"[32] Rosemeade pottery appealed to the buyer of that time and the collector of today. Governor Norman Brunsdale lauded Laura Taylor Hughes in a 1951 Bismarck tribute, "You have taken our clay and designed beautiful pottery which has brought our state recognition in this combination of a valuable resource with a cultural appreciation. You have created in clay our flower, animals, and birds for the enjoyment of our people."[33]

Laura Taylor Hughes chose subjects which continually fascinate people — animals, birds, fish — and modeled original authentic reproductions of their living counterparts. These innovative designs were then accurately hand painted in nature's vivid coloring. Perhaps this is the secret of Rosemeade's success as people in the 1940s, 1950s, and today have identified with these meaningful images of their world.

PRODUCT LINES

Pheasants

Pheasants became synonymous with Rosemeade pottery. Suggested by a salesman, the Chinese ring-necked salt and pepper shakers were described by Laura Taylor as "undoubtedly our best seller."[1] The game bird, "Rosemeade's first wildlife number, was designed for sale in South Dakota. This proved to be an exceptionally popular number, not only in South Dakota, but everywhere that we sold pottery. One dealer wrote us 'Men do not usually buy salt and pepper sets but they do buy your pheasants.'"[2]

A local newspaper also noted that "souvenir birds are proving almost as popular with sportsmen visiting here for the pheasant hunting as the real article,"[3]

with hunters seeking the souvenir natural plumage pheasants. The pheasant salt and pepper shakers were sometimes sold in a small white gift box. A red sticker with black print read, "Congratulations. You have just received North Dakota's most collectible Rosemeade Pottery."

Rosemeade pheasants were also made in such variations as plaques, figurines, and vases. By 1953, more than 500,000 Rosemeade pheasants in nineteen different designs had been sold to an eager public.

All pheasants shown are Chinese ring-necked pheasants unless noted otherwise.

Pheasant TV lamp with head turned to back, 10½" x 11¾", $500.00+. This lamp was also made to order in one plain color.

Pheasant plaques, 6" x 7½" cock and 4¾" x 7" hen, $1,000.00+ pair. "Flying high and colored in all of their natural gay plumage, this pair of Chinese ring-necked pheasants, hen and cock, make an outstanding wall decoration in any room."[4]

Pheasant figurines: 4" x 11½" beak to tail hen, $350.00 – 400.00; 7" x 13" beak to tail cock, $250.00 – 300.00.

Cock pheasant figurine, 5½" x 11" beak to tail, $350.00 – 400.00. This "intermediate size" was considered "better for use on a table as a center-piece than the larger figurine."[5]

Cock pheasant figurine, 9¼" x 14" beak to tail, $350.00 – 400.00.

Cock planter, 3¾" x 9¼", $500.00+.

Pheasant solid figurines: 3" x 3¾" cock with brown tail and 2¾" x 3½" cock with yellow tail, $100.00 – 125.00.

Pheasants: miniature 1¼" x 2½" hen and 2¼" x 2½" cock salt/pepper shakers, $250.00 – 300.00 pair; single hen 1¾" x 3" salt shaker, $20.00 – 25.00; 2¾" x 3¾" cock and 2" x 3" hen salt/pepper shakers, $35.00 – 45.00; 2¾" x 3¾" cock and 2" x 3" hen figurines, $40.00 – 50.00 each; miniature 2½" x 2¼" cock and 1¼" x 2½" hen figurines, $250.00 – 300.00 pair. The 2¾" x 3¾" cock and 2" x 3" hen salt/pepper shakers were the most popular Rosemeade pottery products "measured by the bushel basket when taken out of the kiln."[6]

PRODUCT LINES

Tail-down pheasants, 3" x 4½" cock and 2" x 4½" hen salt/pepper shakers, $75.00 – 100.00 pair; squatty pheasants, 1½" x 5¼" cock and 1" x 4¼" hen figurines, $100.00 – 125.00 pair.

Rare larger salt/pepper shaker versions of squatty pheasants shown with more commonly found versions – larger cock 2" x 6" compared with 1½" x 5¼" and larger hen 4¾" x 1⅜" compared with 1" x 4¼", $200.00 – 225.00 pair of larger version.

Golden Chinese pheasants: 1¾" x 3½" hen and 2¾" x 4" cock salt/pepper shakers, $150.00 – 200.00 pair; 2¾" x 4" cock figurine, $100.00 – 125.00 each.

4" x 4½" pheasants – salt/pepper shakers, $125.00 – 150.00 pair; figurine, $75.00 – 100.00; pick holder, $75.00 – 100.00.

4" x 5" pheasants: pick holder, $75.00 – 100.00 each; figurine, $75.00 – 100.00 each; three flower holders, all with different numbers and different size holes, $75.00 – 100.00 each.

8" oval bowl, black with russet trim to match pheasant, and 4" pheasant flower holder, $125.00 – 150.00 set.

8" oval bowl in natural color and 4" pick holder pheasant, $125.00 – 150.00 set.

9¼" snack tray with 4" pick holder pheasant, $100.00 – 125.00. Also in lime green.

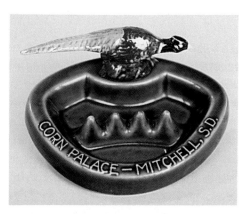

These pheasants were produced as figurines and also used on ashtrays; 1½" x 5¼" figurine, $100.00 – 125.00; 6½" ashtray, $300.00 – 350.00; 2" x 6" figurine, $125.00 – 150.00.

5" ashtray for "CORN PALACE – MITCHELL, S. D." with 1½" x 5¼" pheasant figurine, $150.00 – 200.00. Also advertising "GLACIER PARK."

Pheasant figurine, 2" x 6" on 7" Man's Ashtray, advertising "DAKOTA DAILIES," $300.00 – 350.00 "The Man's Ashtray," in an appeal to men, was produced in heavy black or green ceramic with rounded lines. Laura Taylor observed that "because of its size and capacity" the 7" ashtray "has become a popular gift for men."[7] The "Man's Ashtray" resembled those made for pipe smokers since the early nineteenth century. These were "relatively large with characteristically deep rims so pipes could rest without fear of being knocked over."[8] Smaller and shallower ashtrays evolved as cigarette smoking became more prevalent.

Flying pheasant tray: 3¼" x 6¼" without lettering, $65.00 – 75.00 each: 3¼" x 6¼" with "BISMARCK N. DAK.," $75.00 – 85.00 each; 3¼" x 5¼" without lettering, $65.00 – 75.00 each. Also seen advertising North Dakota cities: BEACH, BELFIELD, BOWBELLS, BOWMAN, CARRINGTON, CEDAR CANTON, DRAKE, DRAYTON, MECHE, MINOT, NEW ENGLAND, PARSHALL, RUGBY, VALLEY CITY. Others in North Dakota: BADLANDS, MEDORA, N. D.; CEDAR CANYON, N. DAK. BAD-LANDS; DEVIL'S LAKE – ANNDEEN'S; DEVIL'S LAKE – MANN'S; HENRY'S DRYGOODS – NECHE, N. D.; "OIL CENTER" WILLISTON, N. D. In South Dakota: BRISTOL, S. DAK.; FLANDREAU, S. DAK.; GAME LODGE, SO. DAK.; HURON, S. DAK.; MADISON, S. DAK.; WESSINGTON SPRINGS, S. DAK.; WOONSOCKET, S. DAK. In Idaho: WALLACE, IDAHO.

Ducks/Geese

Millions of birds are produced yearly in North Dakota's "prairie potholes." Potholes are small depressions in the land created after glaciers scooped out shallow basins. They fill with water from rainstorms or melted snow. These potholes become "a great big duck factory,"[1] as more ducks nest in North Dakota than in any other state except Alaska. "In the spring, between two to three million ducklings hatch in North Dakota's potholes."[2]

North Dakota wetlands are also "crucial to the survival of millions of migratory wildfowl, such as ducks, geese, pelicans, and gulls. The Central Waterfowl Flyway lies over much of North Dakota. Hundreds of thousands fly through, feed, and roost in North Dakota wetlands."[3] Duck hunters travel long distances to hear the whispery rush of a mallard's wings on a quiet frosty autumn morning. Rosemeade Potteries met this market with several products.

Mallard ashtrays, described in an advertisement as "deep and roomy," 3½" x 6½" hen, $325.00 – 350.00; 3½" x 6½" drake, $225.00 – 275.00.

2¾" x 6" drake creamer and 2½" x 6" hen sugar sets. Mallards, $125.00 – 150.00 set; white ducks, $125.00 – 150.00 set; black ducks, $125.00 – 150.00 set. The drake creamers have curly tails.

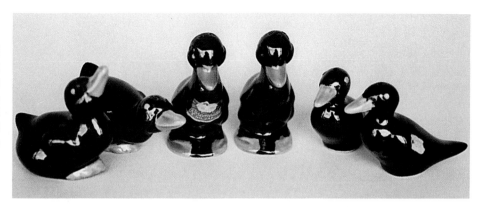

Duckling salt/pepper shakers: one 2½" and the other 2¼", $75.00 – 100.00 pair, also in white or yellow with brown wings and beak; both 2½", $50.00 – 75.00 pair, also in white, bluish-green, maroon, or orange with black beak; both 1¾", $250.00 – 300.00 pair. The black ducks pictured were made for Black Duck, Minnesota.

Mallard duck 1" x 1¾" miniature salt/pepper shakers. Set on left with holes in heads, set on right with holes in backs, $150.00 – 175.00 pair.

Duck 1" x 1¾" miniature figurines – bluebill drake, bluebill hen, mallard drake, two black ducks, $150.00 – 175.00 each.

Mallard plaques: 7" x 7¼" drake, 5½" x 6¼" hen, 6¼" x 6½" drake, and 5½" x 5¾" drake, $2,000.00+ set of four. Three drakes or a drake and hen were also sold together as a set.

Duck pairs, 2" x 3" hens and 3½" x 2½" drakes – mallard salt/pepper shakers, $75.00 – 100.00 pair; mallard figurines, $150.00 – 175.00 pair; white duck salt/pepper shakers, $100.00 – 125.00 pair.

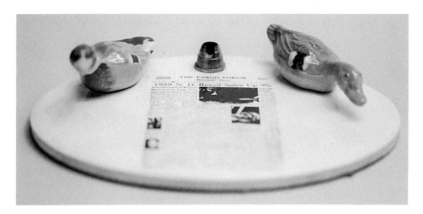

Rare 6" pen holder with mallard ¾" x 2¾" drake and hen figurines and facsimile of *Fargo Forum* December 1959 front page, $700.00+.

Miniature yellow duck figurine on 4½" ashtray, $150.00 – 200.00.

Miniature yellow duck 1¾" x 1½" figurines, $200.00 – 250.00 pair; mallard ¾" x 2¾" figurines, $450.00 – 500.00 pair.

Mallard drake 6¼" x 6" figurine, $250.00 – 300.00.

Mallard 2½" x 3¾" drake – pick holder, $250.00 – 300.00; figurine, $250.00 – 300.00.

Mallard hen covered serving dish, 4½" x 6½", "for candy or cigarettes," $300.00 – 350.00.

Mallard 2½" x 3¾" drake pick holder on 9¼" snack tray, $300.00 – 350.00. Also in blue.

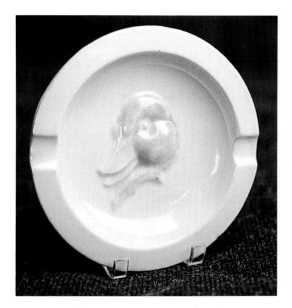

Rare mallard head 4¼" ashtray, $500.00+.

Mallard duck 4" pin, $1,000.00+.

Mallard duck head 2" pin, $1,000.00+.

Miniature 2¼" x 1¼" and 2" x 2" geese figurines, $125.00 – 150.00 pair. Also in yellow.

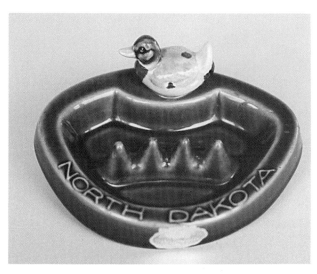

Mallard on 5" advertising ashtray, $175.00 – 225.00.

Mallard on 7" ashtray, $350.00 – 400.00. Also advertising "THE FARGO FORUM."

Fargo Forum mallard 2½" salt/pepper shakers, hen with four holes on back and drake with three holes, incised "FARGO FORUM" mark on bottom, $300.00+ pair. Also in figurines.

Rare squatting mallard figurine on 7" ashtray, $450.00 – 500.00.

Bluebill drake figurine on 5" ashtray, $150.00 – 200.00.

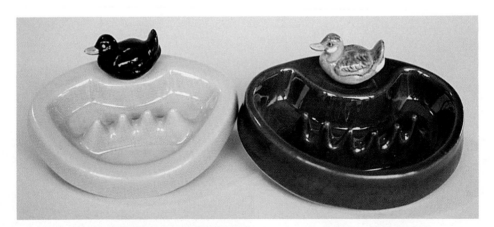

Black duck figurine and bluebill figurine on 5" ashtrays, $150.00 – 200.00 each.

Chickens

Chickens are the most numerous birds in the world, with about 2.3 billion in the United States alone. The "partnership between chicken and man probably first began more than four thousand years ago."[1]

Laura Taylor designed several chickens, including fighting cocks. Cock fighting, outlawed in most of the country, is considered by some "the oldest spectator sport," dating back to the Greeks in 500 B.C.[2]

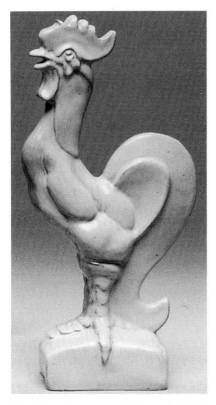

This 8" rooster paperweight, marked "LAT 127," was made by Laura Taylor in 1933 at the University of North Dakota from Mandan clay. It cost $1.10 to make this rooster which sold for $1.80. Also made in green.

Rare rooster TV lamp, 14½" x 7¼", $1,500.00+. Also made in black, brown, and greenish-brown.

Rare flat rooster 7½" x 5" planter, $300.00+.

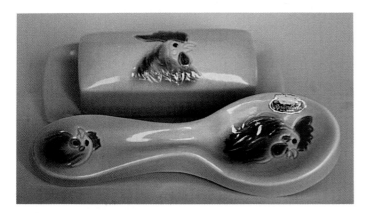

Rooster: ¼ lb. butter dish with 7¾" x 3½" tray and 5¾" x 2¼" cover, $200.00 – 225.00. Also in blue, gold, or green. 8¾" spoon rest, $100.00 – 150.00. Also in blue, gold, or green. The rooster spoon rest and hen and rooster salt/pepper shakers were also sold together as a Range Set.

Hen on a basket, 5½" x 5½", $350.00 – 400.00 each. Also with white basket.

Chicken salt/pepper shakers with 3¼" x 1¾" rooster and 2" x 1¾" hen – white, $85.00 – 100.00 pair; blue feather tip, $85.00 – 100.00 pair.

Chicken salt/pepper shakers, 2½" x 3½" hen with chicks and 3½" x 3¾" rooster, $500.00+ pair.

Salt/pepper shakers: Bantam 1¾" hen and 2¾" rooster, $85.00 – 100.00 pair; 2½" hen and 3¼" rooster, $85.00 – 100.00 pair. The Bantam chickens were made in seven color combinations, including black and white. Other chickens were made in various colors to resemble Rhode Island Reds, Buff Orpingtons, and leghorns.

Chicken salt/pepper shakers in pink, and light blue, 3½" rooster and 2¼" hen, $50.00 – 85.00 pair. Also in black or royal blue.

RIGHT:
Strutting cock 3¾" figurine, $125.00 – 150.00. Base also in black, lilac, or straw color.

LEFT:
Strutting cock 3¾" salt/pepper shakers, $75.00 – 100.00 pair. Also made as figurines; base also in sprout green, lilac, or straw color.

Strutting cock 3¾" x 2¾" pick holder with multiple holes in base and rooster, $100.00 – 125.00.

9¼" snack tray with 3¾" x 2¾" pick holder, $125.00 – 150.00. Also in white, black, blue, or tan.

Strutting cock 3¾" x 2¾" pick holder, $100.00 – 125.00.

Fighting cock figurines, 4¾" x 6" and 5¼" x 6½", $150.00 – 200.00 pair.

Fighting cock figurines, 3" x 4" and 3¼" x 4", black and tan, $200.00 – 250.00 pair. Also in black or black/green.

PRODUCT LINES

Fighting cock 3" and 3¼" salt/pepper shakers, black and green, $150.00 – 200.00 pair.

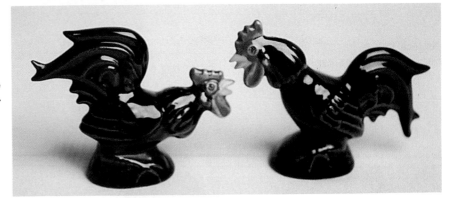

Fighting cock 3" and 3¼" salt/pepper shakers, black, $150.00 – 200.00 pair. Also in black/tan or black/red.

Miniature 1" x 2" and 1½" x 2" fighting cock figurines, $350.00 – 400.00 pair.

LEFT:
Rare fighting cock figurine, 4⅞" x 5", Harvest Gold glaze with "NORTH DAKOTA Rosemeade" mark, $400.00+.

RIGHT:
Rare gloss blue glaze 4⅞" x 5" fighting cock figurine, $400.00+.

Hen figurine on 5" advertising ashtray, $150.00 – 200.00.

Rooster figurine on 5" advertising ashtray, $150.00 – 200.00.

Miniature fighting cock figurine on "MINNESOTA" 5" ashtray, $300.00 – 350.00.

Turkeys

Rosemeade Potteries produced several versions of the turkey, the symbol of Thanksgiving. The turkey, more that any other symbol in America, represents the celebration of harvest and sharing good fortune with others.

Holiday-related collectibles, like these of Thanksgiving, are being sought by growing numbers. A uniquely American holiday, the first national Thanksgiving Day was proclaimed by President Abraham Lincoln in 1864.

Miniature turkeys: salt/pepper shakers, 1½" x 1¾" gobbler and 1" x 2" hen, $175.00 – 225.00 pair; figurines, 1½" x 1¾" gobbler and 1" x 2" hen, $175.00 – 225.00 pair; ¾" x 2" gobbler figurine, $75.00 – 100.00.

Turkeys: 4½" x 5¼" sugar bowl on far left and 3¾" x 6¼" creamer on far right, $125.00 – 150.00 set; 4½" x 4½" covered dish with spoon notch, $150.00 – 200.00; 4½" x 4½" covered dish without spoon notch, $150.00 – 200.00; 3" salt/pepper shakers, $75.00 – 85.00 pair. The notched covered dish is shown with a ceramic spoon, but company literature does not indicate whether it was sold with a spoon. This covered dish was meant for cranberries, candy, nuts, or other purposes. "These pottery numbers in turkey designs are large and roomy and will hold plenty of food for the holiday feast as well as giving the table that festive air."[1]

7" ashtray with turkey gobbler figurine, $375.00 – 425.00. Also made with brown turkey.

9¼" snack tray with 2¼" x 3¼" turkey gobbler figurine, $125.00 – 150.00. Also made in lime green.

6" x 6½" turkeys: pick holder and figurine, $125.00 – 150.00 each.

Rare 5½" turkey gobbler spoon rest, $500.00+.

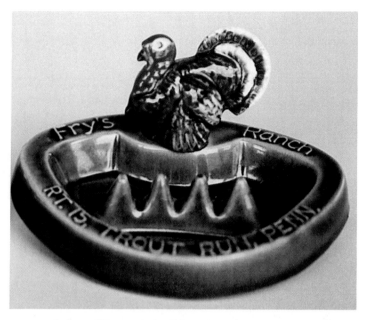

Rare 5½" turkey gobbler spoon rest, $500.00+.

Turkey gobbler on 5" advertising ashtray, $200.00 – 250.00.

Other Birds

"Today, figures of birds are among the most sought after of all ceramic antiques. Entrancing lifelike or highly stylized figures often become coveted collectors' pieces as soon as they go on the market."[1]

Extremely rare peacock figurine, 5¾" x 16", marked "Rosemeade" twice on base. A peacock lamp was also made by Rosemeade.

5½" peacock tea bell, $250.00 – 300.00.

7¾" peacock vase, $250.00 – 300.00.

2" heart pin with peacock motif, $1,000.00+.

Chickadee 1" x 1¾" figurine on 5" ashtray, $250.00 – 300.00.

Baby birds, also called songbirds: chickadee 1" x 1¾" salt/pepper shakers, $250.00 – 300.00 pair; robin 1¼" x 2" salt/pepper shakers, $250.00 – 300.00 pair; goldfinch 1¼" x 2¼" salt/pepper shakers, $250.00 – 300.00 pair; bluebird 1¾" x 1¾" salt/pepper shakers, $250.00 – 300.00. Front row – miniature bluebird 1¼" x 1" figurines, $500.00+ pair; miniature goldfinch ¾" x 1½" figurines, $500.00+ pair. Robins were most popular.

7¾" green peacock vase, $250.00 – 300.00.

Rare seagull plaques, 5¾" wide x 6" long on left, 5¼" x 6½" on right and lower one 6¼" x 5¼", $2,000.00 set. A company promotion described the three styles as "lively seagulls, turning and twisting as in natural flight."

Notched birds (known as cup sitters): 1" x 1¾" chickadee, 1¼" x 2¼" goldfinch, 1½" x 2¼" white bird, 1¼" x 2" robin, and 1¾" x 1¾" bluebird, $150.00 – 200.00 each, except extremely rare white bird. These birds were fashioned to perch on bowls and vases.

Example of cup sitter goldfinch on nut cup.

Goldfinch 1¾" pin, $1,000.00+; blackbird 2¼" pin, $1,000.00+.

2" heart pin with hand-painted bluebird and apple blossom motif, $600.00+. A similar heart-shaped pin was decorated with two birds.

Western meadowlark 2½" pin, $1,000.00+.

LEFT TO RIGHT:
Bird on wood log planter, 3" x 6", $45.00 – 65.00; 6½" x 3" bird on branch with openings for flowers, $45.00 – 65.00; 3½" x 2½" bird with holes in base, $25.00 – 35.00; 3¼" x 3¼" bird candleholder with flower base, $25.00 – 35.00.

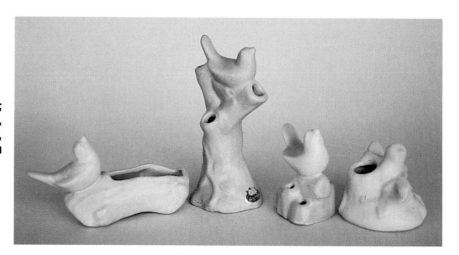

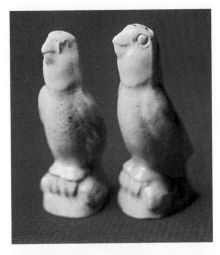

Eagle 2¾" salt/pepper shakers with green body and yellow head, $350.00 – 400.00. Also with brown body and yellow head. Eagle shakers are similar to the parrot shakers, but the eagles look straight ahead and have longer heads.

White eagle 2¾" salt/pepper shakers, $350.00 – 400.00.

Extremely rare bisque 3¼" x 1¾" penguin figurine.

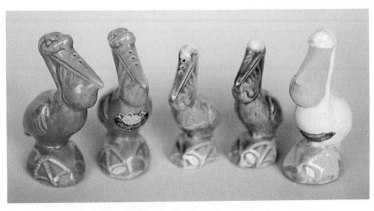

Pelicans: pink 3¼" salt/pepper shakers, $85.00 – 100.00 pair; brown 2¾" salt/pepper shakers, $85.00 – 100.00 pair; and white 3¼" x 3" figurine, $85.00 – 100.00 each. Also in blue, advertised as an "amusing figure with a fish in its oversized beak." According to state tourism literature, Chase Lake, North Dakota, is the world's largest nesting grounds for white pelicans.

Penguin figurines, 1¼" x 2¼" female, 1" x 1¼" baby and 2½" x 1" male, $250.00 – 300.00 set.

Flamingo 3" x 2" and 3¾" x 2" figurines sitting on their high mud nests, $200.00 – 250.00 pair. Also made in salt/pepper shakers.

3¼" flamingo tea bells, pink flamingo on pinkish-green mud nest and white flamingo on gray mud nest, $250.00 – 300.00 each.

Swan 2" salt/pepper shakers, $75.00 – 100.00. Also in black.

Heron 6¾" x 2¾" flower holder with 2" x 8¼" bowl and 2" x 4" candleholders, $175.00 – 200.00 set. Candleholders and bowls were also available in lilac, coral pink, light blue, aqua, moss green, or black. The snowy white heron flower holder base was made in colors to match the bowl and candleholders.

Bobwhite quail 2¼" and 1½" salt/pepper shakers, $50.00 – 75.00 pair.

Swan 4¾" x 5" planters: black gloss, shaded tan matt, green gloss, and blue matt, $35.00 – 65.00 each, made in many colors. "A pair of swans make an artistic and beautiful decoration with or without cut flowers," stated a company advertisement.

2½" and 1¾" Western quail salt/pepper shakers, with topknots of real feathers, $100.00 – 125.00 pair. Ida Prokop may have been the inspiration for Taylor's use of real feathers as Gambel quail topknots on salt and pepper shakers. Prokop was well-known for Dakota Prairie Pictures made from feathers of North Dakota native birds.

Rare 8" x 5¾" flat bird plaque, $300.00+.

These rare bisque flat bird plaques indicate that the plaques were made in other sizes, white clay 5½" x 7¼" and sandy clay 5¼" x 6¾", $300.00+ each.

Roadrunner 2¼" salt/pepper shakers, $150.00 – 200.00. Also in figurines.

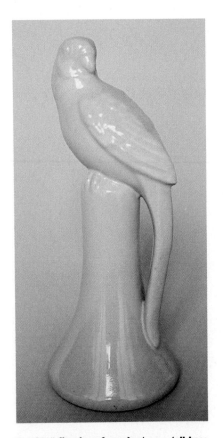

Parakeet 2¼" salt/pepper shakers, shown in three color variations, $200.00 – 250.00 pair.

Parrot 2½" salt/pepper shakers, $150.00 – 175.00 pair.

7" x 2¾" figurine of parakeet on a tall base, $150.00 – 200.00. Also in black.

LEFT:
6" x 2¾" lovebirds on base, $60.00 – 80.00. Also in blue with pink or yellow with light green.

RIGHT:
Rare lovebirds in crescent moon 6¼" x 6¼" wall pocket, $500.00+.

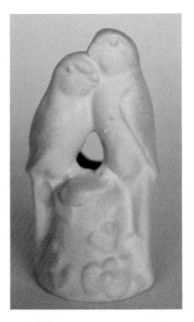

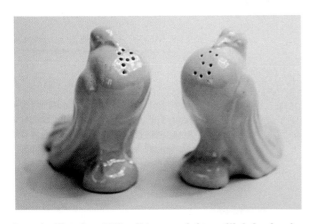

Rare strutting dove 3½" salt/pepper shakers with holes forming initials "S" and "P," $300.00+.

Strutting doves: blue 3½" salt/pepper shakers, $200.00 – 250.00 pair, also in green; single 3" x 2¾" figurine in center, rare, $300.00+.

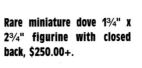

Rare miniature dove 1¾" x 2¾" figurine with closed back, $250.00+.

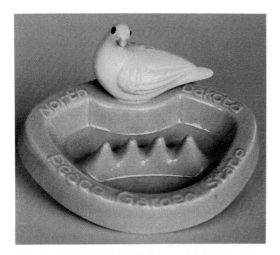

"Dove of Peace" PEACE GARDEN STATE NORTH DAKOTA green ashtray with dove figurine, 5", $300.00 – 350.00 each. Also in pink or blue. Ashtrays like these were given to Miss America contestants in 1956, 1957, and 1958.

Doves: salt/pepper shakers, 1¾" x 2¾", $350.00 – 400.00 pair; nut cups, 1¾" x 2½", $150.00 – 200.00 each.

Dove 4½" x 6¼" planter with one outstretched wing, $125.00 – 150.00.

Dove wall pocket, 4½" x 6¼", $125.00 – 150.00.

Dove planters with two outstretched wings, 3¼" x 5½", in blue, white, and moss green, $125.00 – 150.00 each. Also in lilac and walnut brown and seen as hanging baskets.

Dove 4½" x 6¼" planter with one outstretched wing, $125.00 – 150.00. This planter was produced in bisque with hand-painted highlights so the "pottery clay would show through and highlight the detailed modeling."[2]

Some 3¼" x 5½" dove planters with two outstretched wings were hand painted. This example has the initials "C. D. H." on the bottom, $125.00 – 150.00.

Closed back 4½" x 6¼" dove figurine, $250.00 – 300.00.

Rare Jayhawk, Kansas University mascot salt/pepper shakers – 2½" with wings close to body and 2¼" with wings outstretched, in school colors of maroon and royal blue, $500.00+ each pair. Collectors have given these birds many different names, but company papers indicate they are Jayhawks. Laura Taylor's drawings and bisque ware at the Richland County Historical Museum show two pairs of the mascot, one with wings close to the body and the other with outstretched wings.

Mug, not Rosemeade pottery, which shows the Jayhawk mascot.

Fish/Marine Life

As the pheasants had started their popularity with hunters, so Laura Taylor's fish became popular with fisherman. Realizing that sportsmen wanted recognizable fish, Taylor researched carefully. Her files abound with fish photos and identification information. Attention to detail was such that a local newspaper noted "the large mouth bass is distinguished from the small mouth by the end of his upper jaw which reaches beyond a vertical line drawn through the eye and by the distinct notch between the first and second dorsal fin."[1]

Laura Taylor's choice of fish was calculated on widespread appeal. "With ten popular fish to choose from, we surely must have ones which are caught by your local fisherman." Salt and pepper shakers were made "so that the cottage enthusiast may shake salt on his lake-caught fish from a shaker designed like his catch."[2] Taylor herself observed that those fish on green platters "look natural enough to eat."[3]

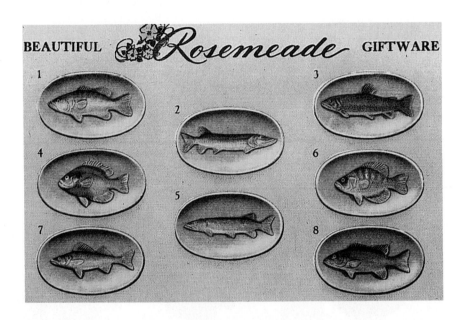

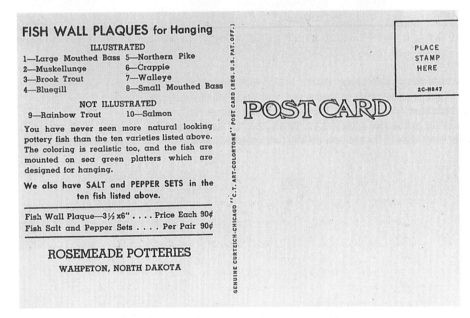

Postcard advertising fish wall plaques. Ten varieties of fish were mounted on "sea green platters... designed for hanging," according to this promotional postcard. Collectors often refer to them as "Fish on a Platter." Some of these fish were available as salt and pepper shakers and figurines.

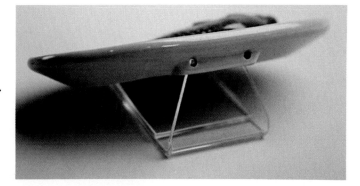

Holes at top of fish plaque for ease in wall hanging.

Bluegill and brook trout 3½" x 6" wall plaques, $225.00 – 275.00 each.

Muskellunge (muskie) and northern pike 3½" x 6" wall plaques, $225.00 – 275.00 each.

Salmon and crappie 3½" x 6" wall plaques, $225.00 – 275.00 each.

Small mouthed bass and large mouthed bass 3½" x 6" wall plaques, $225.00 – 275.00 each.

Rainbow trout and walleye 3½" x 6" wall plaques, $225.00 – 275.00 each. The walleye, Minnesota's eagerly sought state fish, gets its name from its eyes which have a milky appearance like bluish-white marbles.

Walleye 3½" x 6" wall plaque promoting Minot, North Dakota. These plaques were made for different towns. $225.00 – 275.00 each.

Rainbow trout 3½" x 6" wall plaques for Chahinkapa Park. Several Rosemeade items promoted the park where a small gift shop sold Rosemeade pottery. $225.00 – 275.00.

Crappie 3½" x 6" wall plaque, showing variations in painting of the fish as this crappie has very defined scales compared with some others, $225.00 – 275.00.

Some fish have a hump or raised area on the bottom, as shows on the top pair of these brook trout. This hump makes them easier to display. Others, like the lower pair, are flat on the bottom and may be marked with the fish name.

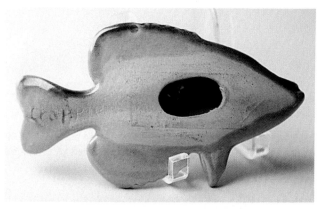

The fish name is often incised into the tail.

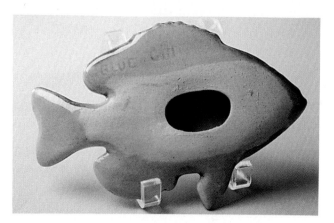

Sometimes the fish name is incised into the fin area.

Brook trout, 1¾" x 5": salt/pepper shakers, flat on bottom with name on tail, $500.00+ pair; figurines, each with a hump on the bottom, $200.00 – 225.00 each.

Bluegill salt/pepper shakers, 2½" x 4": one pair is flat and the other has humps on the bottom, $500.00+ pair.

PRODUCT LINES

Crappie 2¼" x 4" salt/pepper shakers on top row, $500.00+ pair; walleye 1¾" x 4¾" salt/pepper shakers on bottom row, $500.00+ pair.

Northern pike 1¼" x 5" salt/pepper shakers, $500.00+ pair.

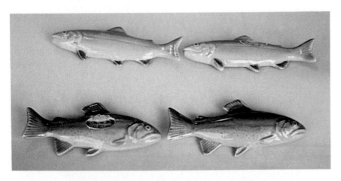

Salmon 1¾" x 5" salt/pepper shakers on top row, $1,000.00+ pair; rainbow trout 2" x 5" salt/pepper shakers on bottom row, $500.00+ pair.

Large mouthed bass 1¾" x 4½" salt/pepper shakers on top row, $500.00+ pair; small mouthed bass 1¾" x 5¾" salt/pepper shakers on bottom row, $500.00+ pair.

Muskellunge 1½" x 5": salt/pepper shakers on top row, $500.00+ pair; salt shaker on bottom row, $150.00 – 200.00.

Walleye figurine on 5" advertising ashtray, $250.00 – 300.00.

Trout figurine and bluegill figurine on 5" ashtrays, $250.00 – 300.00 each.

1½" x 4¼" salt/pepper shakers: bullheads on left in "natural muddy color," $500.00+ pair; catfish on right with "yellow below, dark above," $500.00+ pair.

Miniature fish figurines: 1¼" x 1½" x 1¾" bluegill, $150.00 – 200.00; two northern pike stuck together in firing, ¾" x ¾" x 2¾", $175.00 – 200.00; 1" x ½" x 1½" northern pike, $175.00 – 200.00.

Rainbow trout: 1¼" x 1¾" x 2¾" miniature figurine, $300.00 – 350.00 each; 1" x ½" x 1½" miniature figurine, $300.00 – 350.00 each; 1½" x ¾" x 3¼" salt/pepper shakers, $400.00 – 450.00 pair.

Salt/pepper shakers: 2½" yellow with green dolphins with raised tails, $50.00 – 75.00 pair, also in rose with wine, aqua with blue, sea green with black, or solid yellow; three pairs of 2½" fish, $75.00 – 100.00 pair; 4" blue swordfish, $225.00 – 250.00 pair. The dolphins were advertised as "Waving their sprightly tails, these dolphin salt and pepper sets will add color and zest to a fish dinner."

LEFT:
2½" dolphin figurine, $75.00 – 100.00. Also in other colors.

RIGHT:
Fish 3" x 4¼" bank, $350.00 – 400.00. Also in wine.

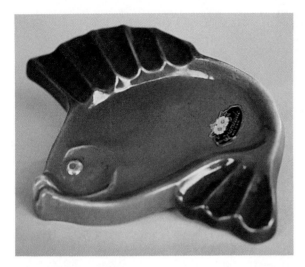

Fish 6¼" ashtray, $100.00 – 125.00. Also in yellow with green, aqua with blue, or bronze.

LEFT: Wine-colored fish pick holder with small holes, 3¾", $75.00 – 100.00. Also in yellow with green. RIGHT: Flower holder with larger holes, aqua with blue, 2¼", $50.00 – 75.00. Also in yellow with green.

Extremely rare 5" tray with fish motif.

2½" fish pin, $1,000.00+.

2½" fish pin, $1,000.00+.

2½" fish pin, $1,000.00+.

2½" fish pin, $1,000.00+.

2½" fish pin, $1,000.00+.

LEFT:
Solid 1¾" x 2¾" frog figurine, $125.00 – 175.00.

RIGHT:
1¼" x 1¼" frog figurine with black painted spots, $100.00 – 125.00.

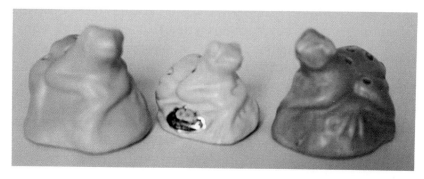

Frog flower holders: blue, 2¾" x 3¼"; yellow, 2" x 2½"; pink, 2¾" x 3¼", $30.00 – 50.00 each.

Sea horses: 10¼" x 3¾" blue flower holder, $200.00 – 250.00; 8" x 3¼" white figurine, $200.00 – 250.00.

Seal figurines, 1⅞" x 2⅛" father, 1¼" x 1¾" mother, ½" x 1¾" baby, brown, $250.00 – 300.00 set; black, $60.00 – 75.00 set.

Rare alligator 1½" x 7¾" figurine, $1,000.00+.

Rare walrus figurine, 4¼" x 6½", marked "as sold in November 1944," $500.00. Also in black and white.

Les Kouba

Les Kouba, nationally renowned wildlife artist, designed and signed three decals used on Rosemeade pottery — "Ring–Necked Pheasant," "Mallard Duck," and "Walleyed Pike." Each appears on the pottery with Kouba's signature. Some pieces list scientific names.

Les Kouba's hunting and fishing motifs, in the *Minneapolis Star Tribune* Sunday newspaper, sparked a marketing idea. Joe McLaughlin, Rosemeade's plant manager, contacted Kouba and inquired about the possibility of making Rosemeade decals from his designs. Kouba declined a fee, replying, "I'd be proud to do it." With this verbal contract, Joe McLaughlin cut the designs out of the newspaper and sent them to the decal company.

The three different decals were used on various Rosemeade items. Ashtrays and mugs were made from white clay or North Dakota sandy clay at the pottery. Tiles, sold as trivets and wall plaques, were purchased from other companies. These tiles were also mounted in purchased walnut, basswood, or maple frames for sale to the public. All decals were applied and fired at Rosemeade Potteries.

After the company closed in 1961, remaining Kouba decals were shipped to Les Kouba in Minneapolis, Minnesota. These decals were used on several objects. Non-Rosemeade pieces can be differentiated because the decals were usually not fired into the clay. Decals were just applied to the surface. Edges can be felt and the decals easily scratched off.

Les Kouba spoke positively of his work with Rosemeade Potteries. "It was a pleasure to be associated with a quality company able to do justice to my work."[1]

Crediting his "realistic depictions to his knowledge of the outdoors,"[2] Les Kouba, who died at the age of 81 in 1998, was noted for painting from real-life experiences. "Authenticity hovers within my art! As I capture, graphically, what I experienced and saw, you feel that you are there."[3]

Les Kouba, wildlife artist, at work.

Kouba "Chinese Ring-Necked Pheasant" print.

Kouba "Mallard Duck" print.

Company promotional photograph of wooden meat and cheese serving tray with 6" decal tile of pheasant.

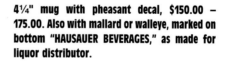

4¾" mugs with decals: "Ring-Necked Pheasant," "Walleyed Pike," "Mallard Duck," $125.00 – 150.00 each.

4¼" mug with pheasant decal, $150.00 – 175.00. Also with mallard or walleye, marked on bottom "HAUSAUER BEVERAGES," as made for liquor distributor.

6" pheasant decal tiles in 8" and 10" wooden frames, $100.00 – 150.00 each. The wooden bowl with handle was made to serve popcorn or fruit, according to Joe McLaughlin.

6" decal tile of pheasant in 10" wooden frame, $100.00 – 150.00.

7¼" square ashtray with pheasant decal, made of white clay at Rosemeade Potteries, $75.00 – 125.00. Also with mallard or walleye.

6" square pheasant decal tile, $75.00 – 125.00.

5" square ashtray with pheasant decal, made of white clay at Rosemeade Pottery, $75.00 – 125.00.

6" pheasant and mallard decal round tile wall plaques, $75.00 – 125.00 each.

10" wooden framed mallard decal on 6" tile, $100.00 – 150.00.

LEFT:
6" square tile with mallard decal,
$75.00 – 125.00.

Framed walleye 6" decal tile on 10" wooden frame,
$100.00 – 150.00. Also on 8" wooden frame.

6" square tile with walleye decal, $75.00 –
125.00.

Wall plaque, 6" round tile with walleye decal,
$75.00 – 125.00.

8" wooden frame with 6" mallard decal tile,
$100.00 – 150.00.

LEFT:
4½" square tile with walleye decal,
$75.00 – 125.00.

RIGHT:
Walleye 6" decal tile mounted in 10"
wooden frame, $100.00 – 150.00.

Floral/Foliage

"Flower painting has been a mainstay of the ceramic decorator's art since the earliest Chinese porcelains and throughout the European tradition."[1] The beauty, fragility, and bright colors of flowers are highlighted in pottery.

As the company trade name, the wild prairie rose was an obvious choice for Rosemeade designs. "This wildflower is part of the natural garden of earth, and no man has a role in its creation."[2] Other Rosemeade floral designs decorate pottery with "flowers and foliage in generous natural profusion."[3]

Prairie rose 4¼" spoon rest, $75.00 – 100.00.

These prairie rose spoon rests were also used for advertising, for example, "BOTTINEAU COUNTY DIAMOND JUBILEE 1959," in lighter pink color, $75.00 – 100.00. Another advertised "Our 50th Anniversary FARMERS STATE BANK FOSSTON, MINN."

Prairie rose 4½" pin trays, one blue and the other white background of pink, yellow, and green, $100.00 – 125.00 each. Also in other colors. This pin tray in a blue-green shade was made for North Dakota Press Association women members' meeting in Wahpeton on August 8 and 9, 1941, "All permanently stamped with date, place and occasion, these pretty and practical souvenirs will be forever reminders."[4]

Extremely rare 5½" hand-thrown prairie rose plate.

Prairie rose 2½" pin, $1,000.00+.

Prairie rose 2½" salt/pepper shakers, $35.00 – 50.00.

8½" prairie rose spoon rest, $75.00 – 100.00; 6" pitcher $75.00 – 100.00; 4¼" pitcher, $50.00 – 75.00.

Prairie rose candleholders, 4½", pastel colors and shades of blue, $150.00 – 200.00 pair.

Prairie rose 2¾" creamer and 2" sugar set, $75.00 – 100.00 set.

Prairie rose 3¾" mug, $65.00 – 85.00. Also with tray as part of TV lunch set.

Prairie rose TV lunch set with 2½" cup and 6¾" tray, $125.00 – 150.00 set.

Extremely rare hand-thrown and hand-painted prairie rose 7½" plate.

5" ashtray with rose design, advertising "FLOWER SHOP – MEHL'S – GREENHOUSES," $250.00 – 300.00.

Extremely rare creme high gloss glaze shoe with hand-painted applied rose motif, 2½" x 4⅞" marked "ANNE K." and "WAHPETON, N.D." with black ink stamp on bottom.

White 5" x 5¼" basket with rose handle, $100.00 – 125.00.

LEFT:
Hand-painted 2" blue heart pin with floral design, $600.00+.

RIGHT:
Hand-painted 2" floral heart pin with ivory background, $600.00+.

Extremely rare white high gloss glaze shoe with hand-painted large applied rose motif, 1½" x 5¼", marked "ANNE K." and "WAHPETON, N.D." with black ink stamp on bottom.

Tulip spoon rests, 5", yellow and blue, $85.00 – 100.00 each. Also in rose and wine colors.

Tulip design matched pieces in wine glaze. FRONT ROW: miniature 1" sugar and 1¼" creamer, $35.00 – 50.00 set; 1¾" salt/pepper shakers, $40.00 – 60.00 pair. BACK ROW: 5½" spoon rest, $85.00 – 100.00; 1¾" sugar and creamer, $150.00 – 175.00 set. Also in rose, yellow, blue, or lilac. An advertisement stated "tulip blooms with their simple cup-like forms and varied colors were the inspiration on these beautifully matched pieces."

Rare dogwood spoon rest, 3½", state flower of North Carolina and Virginia, $300.00+. Also available with pink petals.

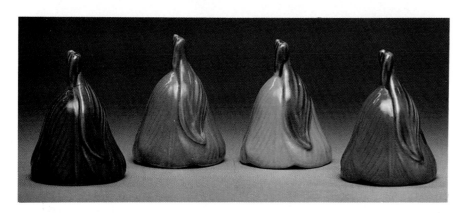

Art Nouveau 3¾" tulip tea bells, wine, blue, yellow, rose, $125.00 – 150.00 each. Art Nouveau, a richly ornamental stylistic movement, emphasized curving flowing lines to realistically depict organic qualities.

Water lily spoon rest, 4¾", $75.00 – 100.00. Also in aqua, rose, or green with white lily blossom.

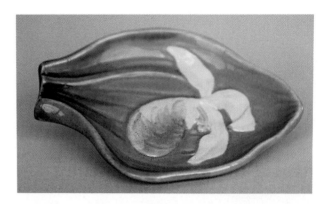

Ladyslipper spoon rest, 4¾", $75.00 – 85.00. The showy ladyslipper, Minnesota's state flower and a member of the orchid family, is a rare wildflower gracing bogs, swamps, and damp woods.

Sunflower spoon rest, 5", Kansas state flower and North Dakota agricultural crop, $125.00 – 150.00.

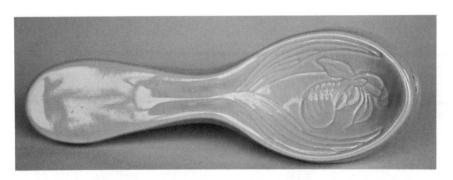

Ladyslipper spoon rest, 8½", $75.00 – 85.00. Also in white with pink and white motif.

Rare golden poppy spoon rest, 3½", state flower of California, $300.00+.

Pansy spoon rests, 4", $75.00 – 100.00 each. Also in color combination of dark brown, light brown, and yellow.

Salt/pepper shakers: barrel cactus 1¾", $60.00 – 70.00 pair; 1¼" sand dollar cactus, $60.00 – 70.00 pair; pincushion 1" cactus, $40.00 – 50.00 pair; 2½" devil's finger cactus $125.00 – 150.00 pair.

Prickly pear cactus spoon rest with flower, 5½", $65.00 – 85.00.

Rare leaves plate, 4½", $250.00+.

4½" leaf motif wall vases, shaded ivory with green and ivory with rose, $50.00 – 75.00 each. Also in turquoise with rose.

Extremely rare hand-thrown vase with hand-painted floral motif, 4¼".

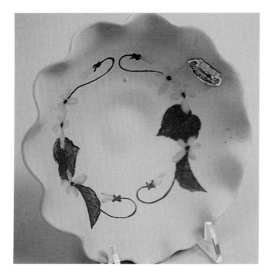

Extremely rare hand-thrown bowl with hand-painted floral and leafage design, 2" x 5½".

PRODUCT LINES

Agricultural

North Dakota is "the nation's number one cash grain state. North Dakota leads the nation in the production of durum and spring wheat."[1] Other state crops, like corn, sorghum, and potatoes, were also featured in Rosemeade products.

Postcard of wheat shocking. "After wheat was cut, it was tied in bundles, the bundles were stacked in piles and called 'shocks.' The bundles were piled to shed rain, then gathered and the grain was separated from the stalks."[2]

Laura Taylor 5¼" plate showing wheat shock, made at the University of North Dakota.

Wheat design. BACK ROW: 8¾" spoon rest, also in yellow, brown, or buff, $75.00 – 100.00; 7" x 5½" desk tray, also in buff, $85.00 – 100.00; 4¼" ashtray, also in buff, $100.00 – 125.00; 5¾" pitcher, $50.00 – 65.00. FRONT ROW: TV lunch set – 6¾" tray with 2¼" cup, $80.00 – 120.00 set; 4¼" pitcher, $50.00 – 65.00; 3" creamer and 2" sugar, $65.00 – 85.00 set; 6¾" tray with 3¾" mug, $80.00 – 120.00 TV lunch set. The 4¼" ashtray was made for male members of the North Dakota Press Association, Wahpeton, N. D., August 8 – 9, 1941, and is marked on the back.

Wheat shock 3¾" salt/pepper shakers, $125.00 – 150.00 pair. Also in green, yellow, or tan. Range Sets of the wheat salt/pepper shakers and spoon rest were marketed.

Wheat motif: 5⅞" green vase, $65.00 – 85.00; 9" white vase, $75.00 – 100.00; 5½" green vase, $65.00 – 85.00; 9¼" dark tan vase, $75.00 – 100.00; 5½" gray vase, $65.00 – 85.00; 7¼" white vase, $65.00 – 85.00.

88

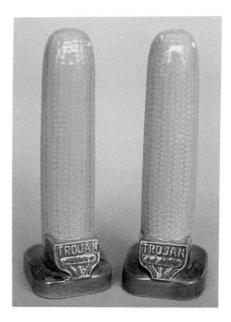

Sweet corn products: 2¼" ear of corn salt/pepper shakers, $35.00 – 50.00 pair; 2" sugar and 2½" creamer, $50.00 – 75.00 set; 4½" ashtray, $35.00 – 50.00. Advertisements stated that these pieces were to be used when "serving that favorite American dish, corn on the cob. The salt and pepper shakers may be used as individual sets. There should be an ashtray for each diner."

Trojan seed corn salt/pepper shakers, 4½", $350.00 – 400.00.

Ear of corn figurine on 5" ashtray, advertising "DEKALB," $225.00 – 250.00.

Potato 1⅝" x 2½" salt/pepper shakers with 4¾" tray, $350.00 – 400.00 set.

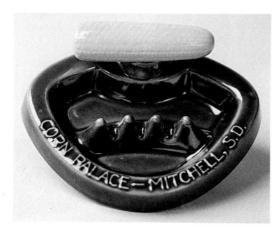

Ear of corn figurine on 5" ashtray, advertising "CORN PALACE – MITCHELL, S.D.," $200.00 – 225.00.

Sorghum figurine on 5" ashtray, advertising "DEKALB HYBRID SORGHUM," $200.00 – 225.00.

Seed potato 2" x 2¾" salt/pepper shakers, advertising "COMPLIMENTS of L. E. TIBERT CO.," a seed company in Voss, North Dakota, $200.00 – 250.00 pair. Advertising salt and pepper shakers were also made for several other seed potato companies in Minnesota and North Dakota, including "N. Dak. State Seed Dept.," and "DE BOER POTATO COMPANY GLENWOOD MINN."

Potato ¾" x 1½" salt/pepper shakers with 3" tray, $400.00 – 450.00 set.

Potato 1½" x 2½" figurine, $100.00 – 125.00.

Extremely rare open 2¼" potato salt dish on 3" tray with the eyes of the potato evident on the tray.

Brussels sprout 1¾" x 1¼" figurine, $50.00 – 75.00.

Vegetable salt/pepper shakers: 1¾" cucumbers, $35.00 – 50.00 pair; 2" peppers $35.00 – 50.00 pair; 1¾" Brussels sprouts, $35.00 – 50.00 pair.

Grape design: 3½" x 5½" planter, $85.00 – 100.00; 3½" x 8½" planter, $85.00 – 100.00; 3½" x 8" cornucopia, $85.00 – 100.00. All three items also in moss green or ivory white.

Grape design on all sides of 4½" square planter, $85.00 – 100.00.

Grape design: 3½" creamer and 3" sugar, made with or without handles, $50.00 – 75.00; 9" two-compartment relish dish, $50.00 – 75.00. Also in pale pink, robin's egg blue, or light green.

5" jam jar with grapes finial, $125.00 – 150.00. Company records indicate that a 3½" jam jar was also made.

5" jam jar with pear finial, $125.00 – 150.00.

5" jam jar with apple finial, $125.00 – 150.00.

RIGHT:
5" jam jar with strawberries finial, $125.00 – 150.00.

LEFT:
5" jam jar with raspberries finial, $125.00 – 150.00. Also with peach finial.

Apple-shaped 6" x 5¼" spoon rests: green is Cambridge, Minnesota souvenir; red celebrating church anniversary, $125.00 – 150.00 each, also in yellow and without advertising.

Extremely rare 3" x 7" hand-painted bowl with cherries design.

Dogs

Dogs are the most popular pet worldwide, with over 50 million in the United States. The domestic dog, which has worked, played, and endured with man for a hundred centuries, has been considered magical and ineffable, "that which is beyond explanation or description."[1] A resilient and adaptable creature, "above all it is a sociable beast."[2]

Since the dog "holds a unique position in human society,"[3] great interest in dog collectibles is understandable. As the dog was a favored creation of Laura Taylor, several breeds were produced as salt and pepper shakers, ashtray figurines, television lamps, and bookends.

In 1950, Laura Taylor modeled twelve different dog heads using design material from *National Geographic Magazines*. Breeds represented were greyhound, chow chow, Chihuahua, Dalmatian, Scottish terrier, Pekinese, English bulldog, bloodhound, English toy spaniel, wire-haired terrier, Boston terrier, and English setter. The dog heads were made into salt and pepper shakers and decorated molded ashtrays. A photograph in the September 1951 *National Geographic Magazine* shows Taylor working on these shakers, after having been sent home to put on a more photogenically colorful smock. According to *North Dakota Horizons*, the line was expected to be a big seller but was not. The dog heads were overproduced. A former employee told of boxes of dog heads, each box holding hundreds of shakers. Since these boxes were on the top of the product bins, a male employee had to be asked to bring a ladder to reach them when needed. Each year at inventory time, employees asked management why the dog heads were still being made. Betty McLaughlin stated that large inventories of the greyhound and English setter dog head salt and pepper shakers remained when the company closed.

Although the thirteenth dog, the cocker spaniel, does not appear in most advertisements, a company promotion sheet stated "Not Illustrated – Cocker Spaniel." According to Laura Taylor, "after receiving many requests for America's most popular dog, we now have the cocker spaniel in a salt and pepper set."[4]

Wolfhound TV lamps, 6" x 11¼", gray, and russet, $500.00+. Also in forest and dark brown.

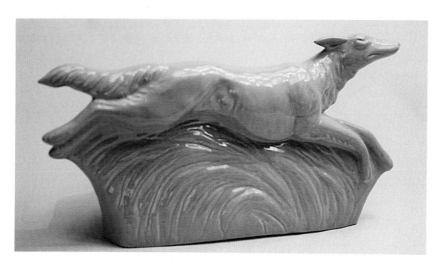
Rare wolfhound, 6" x 11¼" gray planter, $500.00+. "Grace and action characterize this well known dog," stated an ad.

Rare brown 6" x 11¼" wolfhound planter, $500.00+. Also in green.

Back of wolfhound planter.

Art Deco bronze glaze Russian wolfhound bookends, 6½" x 7½", $400.00+ pair. Also in black, wine, and aqua. These wolfhounds were sold as bookends or figurines, some being hollow and others filled. Art Deco, as a popular stylistic movement, turned to streamlined, functional, abstract design.

Solid 3" x 2⅞" begging puppy figurine, $75.00 – 85.00.

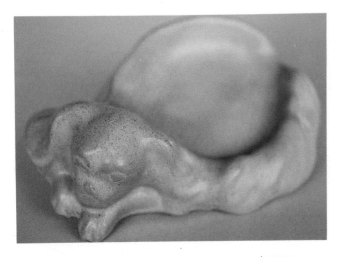

Rare shaded matt cocker spaniel spoon rest, 5¾", $400.00+.

3" begging puppy salt/pepper shakers, $75.00 – 85.00 pair. Also in black, gold, and pink.

Miniature cocker spaniel figurines, 1¾" x ¾" x 1½" and ¾" x 1¼" x 2", two different colors, $500.00+ set of two.

Dog head mark.

Salt/pepper shakers: 2" wire-haired fox terrier with tan ears, $40.00 – 50.00 pair; 2" bluish chow chow, $50.00 – 65.00 pair; 2" russet chow chow, $50.00 – 65.00 pair; 2" wire-haired fox terrier with gray ears, $40.00 – 50.00 pair. The chow chow was also made in gray and the wire-haired fox terrier with brown ears. Company advertising sheets included information about each dog. All descriptions in this section are from these sheets: "WIRE-HAIRED FOX TERRIER: These brave little dogs were developed in England for use in hunting. During a fox hunt they would follow the hound packs and dig out the animals if they went underground. They were also used in hunting badgers, woodchucks, otters, and smaller animals." "CHOW CHOW: The Chow Chow originated in China over 2000 years ago where it was used as a hunting dog. It was also fattened with rice and used for food. The scowl on the Chow's handsome face means 'no nonsense' rather than ill temper."

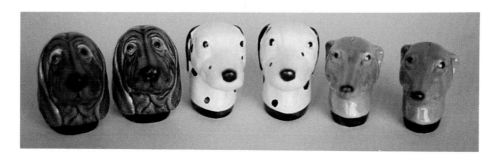

Salt/pepper shakers: 3" bloodhound, $75.00 – 85.00 pair; 3" Dalmatian, $100.00 – 125.00; 2½" greyhound, $35.00 – 50.00 pair. "BLOODHOUND: Bloodhounds are noted for their powers of scent and for their accuracy in following a trail. They are the only animal whose testimony is accepted in an American court of law. Contrary to popular belief, the bloodhound is one of the most gentle of dogs." "DALMATIAN: This handsome dog seems to have an inborn fondness for horses and during the days of coaching he was used as a carriage dog. He has also worked as a shepherd, a circus dog and a hunter. His good manners and his loyalty for his master's family make him an ideal house or guard dog." "GREYHOUND: Greyhounds have been continually bred for speed and endurance and among all dogs they are outstanding in swiftness. They were once used for hunting deer, foxes and other game or kept as companions. Now they are seen mostly at dog racing tracks."

Salt/pepper shakers: 2½" Boston terrier, $250.00 – 300.00 pair; 2½" Scottish terrier with red tongue, $75.00 – 100.00 pair; 2" English bulldog, $100.00 – 125.00 pair; 2" English setter, $35.00 – 50.00 pair. "BOSTON TERRIER: This is one of the few dogs which has been developed in America. First used for pit fighting, they are now kept for house dogs. They have a smart appearance and are good natured and intelligent." "SCOTTISH TERRIER: This is one of the most popular and extensively owned varieties of dogs. They are plucky, good natured, independent and make good companions. The Scottish Terrier takes to hunting furred rather than feathered creatures." "BULLDOG: The name "bulldog" is derived from the dog's former association with the brutal sport of bull-baiting. The Bulldog makes an excellent watch dog and because of his patience and good temper, he is one of the few breeds with whom children may be trusted." "ENGLISH SETTER: The English Setter was developed in England in the 15th century for pointing upland game. It is of aristocratic appearance and lovable disposition. The setter thrives on affection and loves to be in the company of its master, to hunt for him, and to worship him."

Salt/pepper shakers: 2½" Scottish terrier with black tongue, $40.00 – 60.00 pair; 1½" Pekinese, $100.00 – 125.00 each, 2" Chihuahua, $400.00 – 450.00 pair, 1¾" English toy spaniel, $35.00 – 50.00 pair. Also in brown and white. "PEKINESE: The Pekinese originated in China where it was the sacred dog of the Imperial Family. All puppies were brought to the Emperor for personal selection. Although small, these dogs are courageous, bold and hardy." "CHIHUAHUA: Of Mexican origin, this is the smallest of all breeds of dogs. Because of its delicate constitution, it is usually kept for a house pet. Chihuahuas have a saucy expression and they are alert and intelligent." "ENGLISH TOY SPANIEL: These tiny spaniels were long popular in Europe as women's pets and were great favorites with royalty. Even though they are small and delicate, they will bark at the approach of strangers and even attack intruders."

Rare pointers: 2¼" salt/pepper shakers, $800.00+ pair; 2¾" x 4¾" figurine, $600.00+.

Rare thirteenth dog, cocker spaniel: 2" single black pepper shaker, $250.00+; 2" brown salt/pepper shakers, $400.00+ pair.

Dog heads were sold as figurines as well as salt and pepper shakers and on ashtrays.

Rare cocker spaniel figurine on 7" ashtray, $1,000.00+.

Rare pointer figurine on 7" ashtray, $1,000.00+.

English toy spaniel figurine on 7" ashtray, $350.00+.

English bulldog figurine on 7" ashtray, $350.00+.

LEFT: Boston terrier figurine on 7" ashtray, $350.00+. RIGHT: English setter figurine on 7" ashtray, $250.00 – 350.00+.

Cats

Cats are our country's favorite pets with over five million more cats than dogs living in United States' households. Since the ancient Egyptian pharaohs, who revered the domesticated cat before 1900 B.C., the cat has been chronicled in history.

Feline fanciers eagerly seek collectibles of this much-loved animal, which "conjures up in each of our minds our own secret image. Above all, the cat leaves man with a sense of the unknown and mystery."[1] With the feline image a constant worldwide artists' subject, Laura Taylor also created cats.

Rare 6½" kitten in black stocking wall pocket, promoted "for kitchen or children's room," $850.00+.

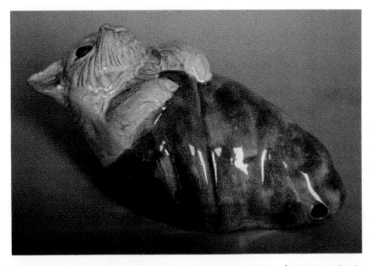

Rare 7" white kitten with lime green stocking string holder, $850.00+. Also in black, blue, or white stocking.

Rare 6½" white kitten in blue stocking wall pocket, $850.00+.

Rare 8" white cat on 4¾" x 4½" base, $1,000.00+.

LEFT:
Rare 8" blue cat on 4¾" x 4½" base, $1,000.00+.

Kitten salt/pepper shakers, 2¼", $50.00 – 75.00 pair. Kitten figurines, 2" x 2", $35.00 – 50.00 each.

Cats: 3½" pink salt/pepper shakers, $75.00 – 100.00 pair; 3½" blue salt/ pepper shakers, $75.00 – 100.00 pair; 2¾" Siamese salt/pepper shakers, $75.00 – 100.00 pair; 2¾" black salt/ pepper shakers, $75.00 – 100.00 pair; 3½" x 2¼" black and white figurines, $60.00 – 75.00 each; 3½" tan figurine, $60.00 – 75.00; 3½" blue figurine, also in green, $60.00 – 75.00.

Horses

Equine art continues to attract collectors. "Whether it is the awesomeness of its power and speed, the gracefulness of its lines, or the mystery of its association with man (at once submissive and free spirited), the horse has aroused the fiercest emotions and the most splendid artistic responses."[1] Rosemeade's equestrian sculpture reflected North Dakota's Western orientation with the importance of the horse to cowboys, ranchers, and Native Americans.

Talented sculptress Vera Gethman created spirited horses using wild horses roaming near her Badlands ranch home as live models. As Laura Taylor Hughes described Gethman's artistic skills, "She gives animation to clay in her hands and distills the nostrils of the animal with the rarefied air of the plateau regions of the state."[2]

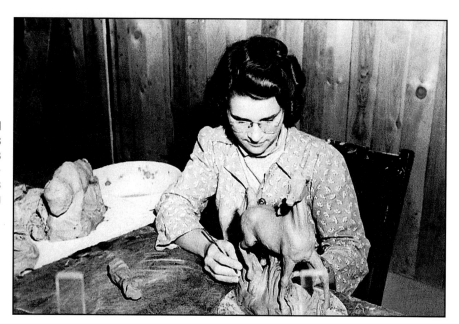

9½" x 8¾" bronze horse figurine with cut-out foliage, $500.00+. This horse was also made in palomino color, chestnut, and black. When the movie *The Red Stallion* was scheduled to show at the Wahpeton Theatre, a one-of-a-kind red horse with white markings was made using this model. The horse was displayed at the theater and is now on exhibit at the Richland County Historical Museum. Another version of this horse, with a white marking on its head and black body, is part of a private collection.

Horse TV lamps, 9½" x 8¾", $500.00+ each. Also in brown.

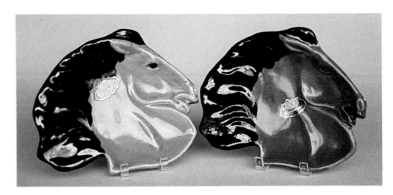

Horse spoon rests, 5¾", blue and pink, $125.00 – 175.00 each.

Rare horse lamp, 9½" x 8¾", $800.00+.

Solid circus horse figurine, 4¼" x 4¼", $350.00 – 400.00.

Circus horse planters, 5" x 6½", light blue, bright blue, and pink, $75.00 – 100.00 each.

Solid horse figurine, 4¼" x 3", also in blue, $250.00 – 300.00.

Horse figurines with heads in different positions, 6¼" x 4¼" black gloss; 6¼" x 4¼" blue gloss; 5½" x 4¾" reddish; 5¾" x 4½" black matt; 4¾" x 5¼" tan, $150.00 – 200.00 each.

Colts: blue salt/pepper shakers, 2½" x 2½" and 2½" x 2¾", $75.00 – 85.00 pair; blue miniature figurines, 2" x 2" and 1¼" x 2½", $125.00 – 150.00 each; palomino figurines, 2½" x 2½" and 2½" x 2¾", $50.00 – 75.00 each. These horses were also available in pink and green.

5" ashtrays with palomino colt figurines, $150.00 – 200.00 each.

Palomino horse head salt/pepper shakers, 1½", $50.00 – 75.00 pair. Also in black, white, and bronze. This design was advertised as "gentle but spirited-looking horse with flowing mane."

Horse design: TV lunch set with 6¾" tray and 3¾" mug, $75.00 – 100.00 set; 4¼" pitcher, $40.00 - 60.00; 5¾" pitcher, $40.00 – 60.00; 6¾" tray with 2¼" cup, $75.00 – 100.00 TV lunch set; 2" sugar and 3" creamer, $40.00 – 60.00 set. Besides the TV lamp, another influence of television in the decade of the 1950s was the "TV tray" "with matching mug to permit the TV viewer to enjoy a favorite program while munching a sandwich and sipping a beverage," as described in a company advertisement.

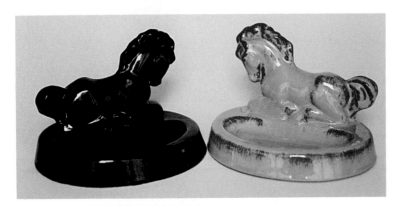

Ponies on 7" ashtrays, $250.00 – 300.00 each.

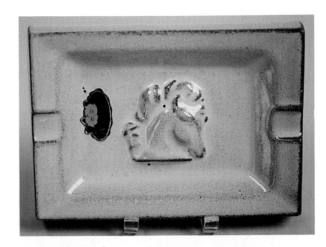

Extremely rare 4¾" horse cream pitcher with unusual glaze.

Pony figurine, 3¾" x 6", $250.00 – 300.00.

5¼" ashtray with embossed horse head motif, $150.00 – 200.00. Also in gold.

5" cigarette box with embossed horse design, $250.00 – 300.00. Also in tan.

White horse head plaque with ears extended, 2½" x 4", $300.00 – 400.00. Also in tan.

Horse head 4½" x 6" plaques: bronze with mane to side and tan with mane down front of head, $300.00 – 400.00 each. Also in pink and black.

Brown horse head plaque with ears lying flat, 2½" x 4", $300.00 – 400.00.

3½" horse head pin, $1,000.00+.

3½" horse head pin, $1,000.00+.

Farm Animals

"Animals found on the farm hold a special appeal. Because of all the products they supply, farm animals create a more bountiful world for all of us."[1]

Laura Taylor created many lifelike barnyard animals from the mule to the pig. Since, "nearly two million head of cattle are produced on North Dakota grass"[2] every year, Rosemeade cattle are popular collectibles.

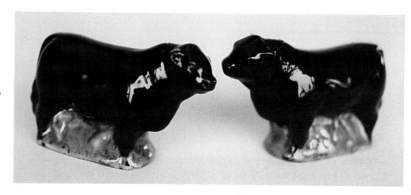

Black Angus 1¾" salt/pepper shakers, $300.00 – 350.00 pair. Also in figurines.

1¾" Black Angus figure on 7¾" feed store ashtray, $400.00+.

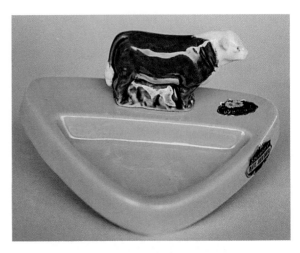

Hereford figure on 6¼" triangular ashtray, $400.00+.

Hereford figure on First State Bank of Minnesota 6½" ashtray, $400.00+.

Ox head salt/pepper shakers, 2¼", $75.00 – 100.00 pair; Brahman bulls salt/pepper shakers, 1¾", $350.00 – 400.00 pair.

5" plain ashtrays with Holstein cow figure, $350.00 – 400.00; Guernsey cow figure, $350.00 – 400.00.

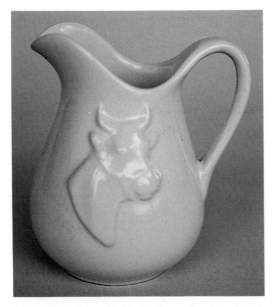

Cow pitcher, 4⅜", advertising "LINDALE CREAMERY WAHPETON N. DAK." on back, $100.00 – 125.00.

1¾" cow and bull salt/pepper shakers, $150.00 – 200.00 pair. Also in red or brown.

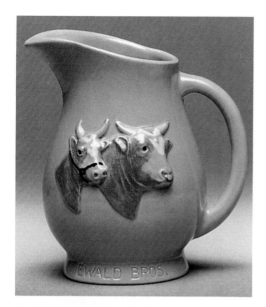

Ewald Dairy 6" pitcher made to advertise Minneapolis dairy, $125.00 – 150.00. Also in two other sizes.

Pig salt/pepper shakers, 3¾", $125.00 – 150.00 pair. Also in blue or brown.

Hampshire pig with white band spoon rest, 6", $150.00 – 175.00 pair. Also in brown.

Extremely rare lamb figurine, 2½" x 3", solid and handmade.

LEFT:
Lamb planter, 6" x 6½", $150.00 – 200.00.

RIGHT:
Extremely rare lamb, 6" x 6½" figurine. This piece may have been meant to be a doorstop as it is very heavy and is filled with a rattling material.

4¼" x 5¼" figurine of mule standing with cactus, $250.00 – 300.00; brown mule in front of planter, 4¾" x 6", $250.00 – 300.00; black mule figurine, 4" x 6", $250.00 – 300.00.

Kid goat planter, 5¼" x 3½", $75.00 – 100.00.

Mule head salt/pepper shakers, 2½", $60.00 – 80.00 pair. "With a Roman nose, ears laid back and teeth bared, this is a typically stubborn looking mule," stated an ad.

Extremely rare 4" x 2½" mule figurine with crossed ears. Also made in Harvest Gold and green.

3½" x 5" mule figurine, $250.00 – 300.00. Another size, 4¾", was also available. The mules were also made in natural brown or white. "Enough to make a three-mule train," as advertised in the August 1950 *The Gift and Art Buyer*.

Deer

Laura Taylor's deer motifs were in such demand that by 1952 they were described in the local newspaper as "among the most popular items ever produced at the local pottery and probably will give the well-known pheasant a bit of a contest." Deer, long admired for their beauty, graceful movements, speed, and jumping ability, had wide sales appeal in the Midwest and many areas of the country.

One of Laura's earliest figurines was a "graceful deer showing the long legs characteristic of the animal."[1] In 1949, prancing fawns "dressed up with holly boughs" pulled a sleigh as "a perfect holiday arrangement for mantel or table decoration," in a company advertisement.

The same arrangement was used for the Wahpeton Pottery Company Christmas card that year.

Bambi, a fawn "appealing as the spirit of Christmas itself,"[2] was born in 1952. Hand-painted in a naturalistic fawn color with a white chest and spots, Laura added a touch of whimsy, coal black eyes. Park Commissioner Robert Hughes pointed out this divergence from nature but "his artistic wife insisted that they show up better that way." Bambi items, figurines, and salt and pepper shakers enjoyed brisk sales, especially during the holiday season. The Bambi motif was also used for their 1952 Christmas card, sending greetings from the pottery.

1949 Wahpeton Pottery Company Christmas card.

Dutch sleigh planters, 4" x 5¼", $75.00 – 100.00 each. A Dutch sleigh was the type pushed on the ice in the Netherlands.

3¾" x 3" tan and brown prancing fawns: salt/pepper shakers, $100.00 – 150.00 pair; figurine, $100.00 – 150.00. This prancing fawn was made with a pierced base for use as a flower holder and with a slot for use as a placecard holder.

Prancing fawns, gray with brown markings, 3¾" x 3", $150.00 – 175.00 pair.

1952 company Christmas card.

Bambi deer sets. BACK ROW: 2½" x 2¾" and 1¼" x 3½" salt/pepper shakers, $100.00 – 125.00 pair; figurines, $125.00 – 150.00 each. FRONT ROW: Miniature figurines, ¾" x 2¼" and 1½" x 1¾", $250.00+ each.

Bambi deer figurines on 5" ashtrays, $175.00 – 200.00 each. The deer on the right also appeared on a "DULUTH MINNESOTA" ashtray.

Bambi deer figurines on 5" triangular ashtray, $125.00 – 150.00.

Fawn TV lamp with evergreen base, 9½" x 11", $500.00+. Also in pink.

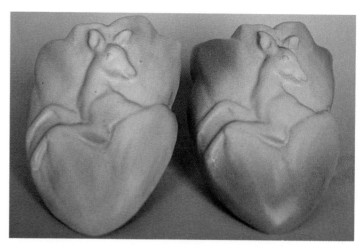

5" deer wall pockets, aqua and pink, $40.00 – 60.00 each. Also in high gloss shaded blue.

3¼" x 3¾" deer planters in blue and pink, $50.00 – 75.00 each. Also in tan with pink roses. 3¾" x 5¼" shaded yellow to green matt planter, $50.00 – 75.00. Also in blue shaded to green and bronze.

Deer 7¾" x 7¾" figurine, $100.00 – 125.00. Also in blue.

Deer vases: 8¼" gloss glaze and 7¾" matt glaze, $35.00 – 75.00 each.

Prancing fawn figurine, 6¼" x 5½", $125.00 – 175.00.

Prancing fawn 6¼" x 5½" flower holder in 7½" low bowl, $175.00 – 225.00 set. The low bowl also came in black, wine, and blue.

Prancing fawn flower holders, 6¼" x 5½", with different number and placement of holes, $125.00 – 175.00 each.

Bison

"Perhaps no animal in the history of any nation has ever played a more important role than the American bison,"[1] "an icon of the American West, partly from its size and partly from its connection with people."[2] Bison is the correct name for North America's largest animal, part of the bovine family of mammals along with domestic cattle. Early French explorers mistakenly called this majestic creature "buffalo," a term which continued in usage. The Asian water buffalo and African Cape buffalo are true buffalo.

The source of life for Plains Native Americans, bison provided food, shelter, and clothes and became a symbol of the Great Spirit. Sixty to seventy-five million bison roamed North America's western plains in the early 1800s. The westward expansion movement brought on rapid bison decline to the verge of extinction. Today, due to the efforts of many Americans, thousands of bison again thrive on private ranches and in state and national parks.

As one of our country's best-known animals, the bison motif has adorned numerous objects and institutions. Rosemeade Potteries made several bison versions from the Jamestown Monument to the North Dakota State University mascot.

Green mottled matt glaze bowl with incised decorative rim and two bison buttresses made by Laura Taylor at the University of North Dakota.

As a student at UND in 1932, Laura Taylor made this bison figurine, marking the base with her name and date.

Solid matt glaze bison figurines, 2½" x 3½", $100.00 – 125.00 each.

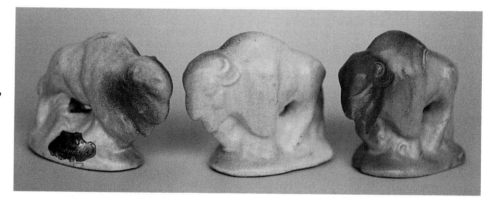

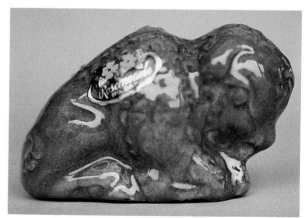

Solid 2½" x 3½" bison figurines, black gloss glaze and bronze gloss glaze, $100.00 – 150.00 each.

Rare solid bison figurine, lying down, 2" x 3¾", $500.00+.

Three bison figurines, 6" x 6¼", in brown matt, dark brown matt, and bronze gloss glazes, $300.00 - 400.00 each.

The brown gloss glaze bison figurine, 3½" x 5", was made for Jamestown, North Dakota, from sandy colored clay, $250.00 - 300.00. One side of the base mark reads "WORLD'S LARGEST BUFFALO" and the other side, "JAMESTOWN, N. D." Jamestown, known as the "Buffalo City," is the home of "The World's Largest Buffalo," a sixty-ton sculpture standing watch on a hill clearly visible from Highway I-94. A live buffalo herd, including a rare white albino buffalo, White Cloud, grazes near the National Buffalo Museum, dedicated to the history of the American Bison. The center brown gloss bison with head turned, $400.00 – 450.00, is 4" x 5½". On the right is a dark brown gloss glaze bison figurine, $250.00 – 300.00. Because this figurine was made of white clay, it measures 4" x 5½", larger than the bison on the left due to less clay shrinkage. Rosemeade Potteries produced this white clay bison for Jamestown's 1958 centennial. As earlier bison molds had been lost by this time, Joe McLaughlin said that a new mold was made.

Yellow 2½" x 2½" bison with "FARGO" on one side and "N.D.A.C." on the other side, $175.00 – 200.00.

2½" x 2½" bison salt/pepper shakers, $100.00 – 150.00 pair; three figurines, $100.00 – 125.00 each.

Bison banks, with base slogan of "WORLD'S LARGEST BUFFALO" on one side and "JAMESTOWN, N. D." on the other, $300.00 – 400.00 each. The brown bank on the left is 3½" x 5" and made from sandy clay. The darker brown bank on the right is made from white clay and measures 4" x 5½".

Bison bookends, 6" x 6¼", $600.00+ pair. Advertised as "Weighed and the bottoms are finished with felt," these bookends "will really hold books." These bookends were marked "N.D.A.C." on base as they were made for the North Dakota Agricultural College in Fargo. The college name was changed to the North Dakota State University of Agriculture and Applied Science in 1961.

Other Wildlife

Enjoyment of wildlife is universal, a reminder "that we share our planet Earth with a huge number of other creatures. The very wildness also attracts us. There is something special about animals that are wild and free — that don't depend on humans and still live as they have for thousands or even millions of years"[1]

The Wahpeton Pottery Company and Rosemeade Potteries created a wide variety of wildlife. Bears and elephants, well represented in Rosemeade pottery, have become particularly collectible in recent years.

"Snarling Wildcats" salt/pepper shakers, 1½" x 4¼", $600.00+ pair. This animal is sometimes called a puma or mountain lion by collectors, but company records don't mention a mountain lion or puma being produced. However, the "Snarling Wildcat" shows up on several company stock listing sheets. Also, the mountain lion is a solid tan color whereas the wildcat has a mottled colored coat similar to this Rosemeade version. The wildcat, sometimes called bobcat, is native to Northern states, a "symbol of the wild."[2] Since the wildcat was the mascot of Wahpeton's State College of Science, Laura Taylor may have directed this animal toward that market.

"Snarling Wildcat" figurine on 5" ashtray, $400.00 – 450.00. Tiger kitten figure on 5" ashtray, $300.00 – 350.00.

Tiger kitten miniature figurines, 1" x 2¾" and 1¼" x 2", $500.00+ pair.

Extremely rare coyote plaque, 3" x 3½". The coyote is South Dakota's state animal, whose long melancholy wail reaches across the prairie.

Panther TV lamps, 7" x 13", pink, forest green, and black, $500.00+ each. Also in bronze.

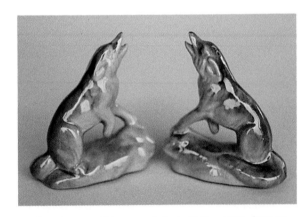

Howling coyote salt/pepper shakers, 3¼" x 2¾", $250.00 – 300.00 pair.

Howling coyote figurines, 4½" x 3⅞" $250.00 – 300.00 each.

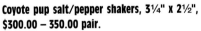

Coyote pup salt/pepper shakers, 3¼" x 2½", $300.00 – 350.00 pair.

Mountain goat and baby wall pockets, 4½" x 5¾", maroon base and gray base, $500.00+ each. Rosemeade mountain goats display the characteristic bearded chin and backward-curving black horns.

Mountain goat, 3¼" x 3⅛" figurine with plastic horns glued into spaces left in clay, $225.00 – 275.00. This is the first known time that another material, like plastic, was used on a Rosemeade product.

Single salt shaker with blue mountain goat on green base, 2¼", $75.00 – 100.00.

Mountain goat baby figurine with no horns or spaces for horns, 3¼" x 3½", $150.00 – 175.00.

Mountain goat 2" pin with maroon base, $1,000.00+. Also made in ram's head shape.

2¼" x 2¼" mountain goats: salt/pepper shakers on blue bases and maroon bases, $125.00 – 150.00 pair; figurine on maroon base, $150.00 – 175.00.

Mountain goat 2" pin with aqua base, $1,000.00+.

Red fox salt/pepper shakers, 1" x 3¼" and 1¾" x 1¾", $350.00 – 400.00 pair; figurines, $350.00 – 400.00 pair.

LEFT: Red fox planter, 2¾" x 3½", made for "VADA'S STEAK HOUSE," with black ink stamp mark on bottom with Rosemeade sticker. RIGHT: Same style planter with Rosemeade black ink stamp but not for VADA'S. $500.00+ each.

Two rare solid figurines of two foxes together, 2¼" x 3¼", $600.00+ each.

Two 5" ashtrays with red fox figurines, $200.00 – 250.00 each. This lying fox was also used on a "COLUMBIA FALLS, MONT." ashtray.

Raccoon figurine on 5" triangular ashtray, $125.00 – 150.00.

Raccoons: miniature figurines, 1" x 2½" and 1¼" x 1½", $250.00 – 300.00 pair; salt/pepper shakers, 1¼" x 2¾" and 1¾" x 2", $150.00 – 200.00 pair; figurines, 1¾" x 2" and 1¼" x 2¾", $200.00 – 250.00 pair.

Skunks: 2¾" salt/pepper shakers, $40.00 – 60.00 pair, 2¼" salt/pepper shakers, $40.00 – 60.00 pair; miniature 1½" and ¾" salt/pepper shakers, $100.00 – 125.00 pair; miniature ¾" and 1½" figurines, $40.00 – 60.00 each; 2¾" figurines, $50.00 – 70.00 each.

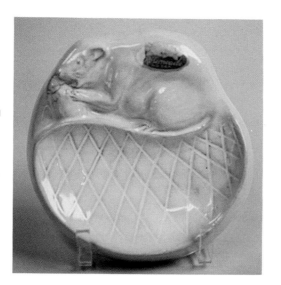
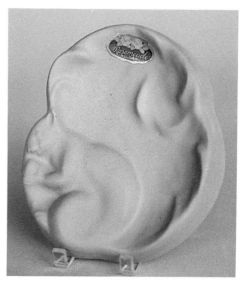

LEFT:
Extremely rare 4½" spoon rest with beaver motif.

RIGHT:
Extremely rare squirrel 4¼" dish, shaded matt glaze.

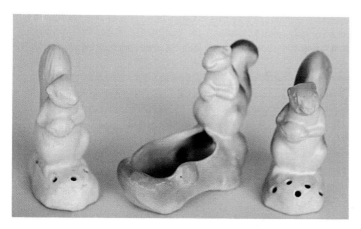

Squirrels: two 4½" flower holders with different number holes, $40.00 – 60.00 each; 4¼" x 5¾" planter, $40.00 – 60.00. Planter also in blue.

Squirrel pin, 2¾", $1,000.00+.

4" squirrel flower holder with mark "NORTH DAKOTA Rosemeade," $125.00 – 150.00.

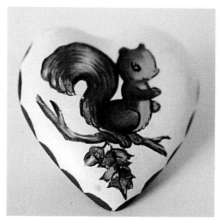

Hand-painted heart pin with squirrel motif on white background, 2", $600.00+.

Squirrel heart pin on blue background, 2", $600.00+.

Extremely rare brown flickertail (Richardson's ground squirrel) plaque, 5¼".

Badger figurine on 5" ashtray, "Badger State – WISCONSIN," $500.00+. The badger is Wisconsin's state animal.

Gopher figurine on 5" ashtray, "GOPHER STATE – MINNESOTA," $150.00 – 200.00. Minnesota's state animal is the gopher.

Flickertails (Richardson's ground squirrels): 4" tan salt/pepper shakers, $75.00 – 100.00 pair; 2¼" tan salt/pepper shakers, $60.00 – 85.00 pair; 2¼" gray salt/pepper shakers, $150.00 – 200.00 pair; 4" x 1¾" tan figurine, $40.00 – 80.00; 3¾" x 1¼" tan figurine, $40.00 – 80.00; 2¼" x 1" tan figurine, $40.00 – 80.00.

There is confusion among collectors regarding the name of these Rosemeade animals. The company information stated that "the flickertail is more commonly hunted as the gopher" and company stock pages list this animal as "gopher or ground squirrel-striped." Richardson's ground squirrels or flickertails are "commonly but wrongly called gophers."[3] The pose of this animal is that of the Richardson's ground squirrel, which "stands up straight on its heels if alarmed when foraging,"[4] not that of a gopher. The Rosemeade Company acknowledged that these flickertails were not painted true to their natural "smoky gray coats which blends into their Northern prairie home."[5] Instead, the Rosemeade versions were "touched up by the artist as to stripes and spots a bit more than the protective coloring in nature."[6]

Prairie dogs: 2½" salt/pepper shakers, $50.00 – 75.00 pair; figurines, 1¼" x 1" and ¾" x 1¼", $50.00 – 75.00 each. Prairie dogs are yellow in color with small ears, short tails, and short, muscular legs. The poses of these Rosemeade renditions are typical of prairie dogs.

Badger salt/pepper shakers, 1" x 2¾", $600.00+ pair.

Figurine of gopher with nut, 1½" x 2", $50.00 – 75.00.

Rabbit cotton dispenser, 4¾" x 2½", $150.00 – 200.00.

Back of rabbit cotton dispenser.

Rabbit figurine, 4¾" x 2½", $100.00 – 150.00.

4½" watering pot with rabbit motif, holes in spout, $75.00 – 100.00. Also in gold or turquoise.

4½" rabbit motif watering pot with open spout, $75.00 – 100.00. Also in gold or rose.

Jackrabbit solid figurine, 3¼" x 1¾", $250.00 – 300.00.

Jackrabbits: pink 2½" x 3" figurine, $250.00 – 300.00; 2½" gray pepper shaker, $100.00 – 125.00 single; 1¾" gray salt/pepper shakers, also in wine, pink, or blue, $125.00 – 150.00 pair. The jackrabbit, more properly known as a hare, has large ears and long hind legs permitting "leaps across the ground at great speed." [7]

2½" jackrabbit pin, $1,000.00+.

Mice salt/pepper shakers, 1¾" x 1" and 1¼" x 2", $25.00 – 50.00 pair; 1" x 1¼" and 1½" x 1", $25.00 – 50.00 pair. Also as figurines.

Mouse cheese serving plate, 6", $75.00 – 100.00.

LEFT:
Mouse figurine on 5" triangular ashtray, $125.00 – 150.00.

RIGHT:
Mouse figurine on 5" ashtray, $125.00 – 150.00.

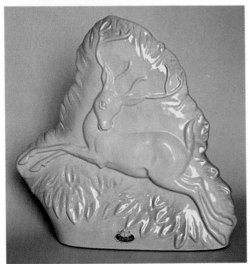

Hippopotamus solid figurines, 2¼" x 3½", $300.00 – 350.00 each.

Wapiti (American elk) TV lamp, 10" x 11¼", $600.00+. Also in pearl gray, pink and white, russet, sprout green, or white. "About 200 years ago, prairie states had large herds of wapiti — wild elk — living in the wide-open grasslands."[8] This lamp highlights the long and wide antlers of the bull elk.

Hippopotamus bank, 2¾" x 5¾", $500.00+.

Hippopotamus bank, 2¾" x 5¾", $500.00+. Also in maroon.

Rhinoceros bank, 3½" x 6½", $600.00+.

Rhinoceros bank, 3½" x 6½", $600.00+. Also in maroon.

Extremely rare 9½" giraffe figurines.

Rare bisque hand-painted zebra salt/pepper shakers, 4" x 1½" $1,000.00+ pair; solid figurine, $500.00+.

Rare miniature monkeys, 1¾", "Hear No Evil, See No Evil, Say No Evil," $1,500.00+ set.

3¼" kangaroo salt/pepper shakers, $50.00 – 75.00 pair; figurine, $75.00 – 100.00.

Monkey solid figurine, 3" x 2", $500.00+. The hand-formed model for this piece is on page 24.

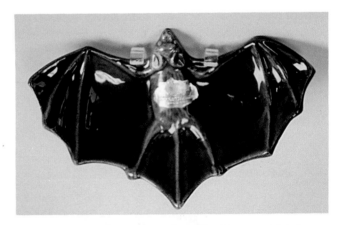

Kangaroo salt/pepper shakers, 2¾" x 3" male, 2¼" x 2½" mother with joey in pocket, $350.00+ pair.

Kangaroo planter, 4¾" x 6", $100.00 – 125.00.

Rare bat spoon rest, 3½" width x 5¾" length, $500.00+. This bat spoon rest was made for sale at Carlsbad Caverns, Carlsbad, New Mexico, as a souvenir. Laura Taylor mentions her concern in a 1951 letter, "I'm not well enough acquainted with the creatures to know if this is the right shade or not."[9]

Solid gloss elephant with trunk down, 2¼" x 2¾", $200.00 – 250.00. Also in other colors.

Miniature 1½" x 1½" elephant figurines, $100.00 – 125.00 pair.

Solid matt elephant with trunk up, 2¾" x 2¾", $100.00 – 150.00. Also in green or blue.

5¾" elephant spoon rest, aqua, without hole by trunk; wine and aqua with hole by trunk, $125.00 – 150.00 each. Also in rose.

Aqua elephant bank, 4¼" x 3", $500.00+. Also in rose or wine.

5" x 5¼" blue elephant planter, tan planter, pink with open gondola, blue closed figurine, wine with flower frog holes, $125.00 – 150.00 each.

4¼" elephant incense burners, rose and aqua, $150.00 – 200.00 each. Also in wine.

4¼" elephant tea bells, rose and aqua, $150.00 – 200.00 each. Also in wine.

Elephant planter with flower holder holes, 5½" x 4¾", $75.00 – 100.00.

2¾" elephants: salt/pepper shakers, gray, aqua, rose, tan, $50.00 – 75.00 pair. Also in maroon or black. Solid figurines in black and rose, $75.00 – 85.00 each. Also in maroon, gray, aqua, or tan.

Miniature 1½" x 1½" elephant figurine on 5" triangular ashtray, $200.00 – 250.00.

Miniature 1½" x 1½" elephant figure on 7" ashtray, $200.00 – 250.00.

Bear banks, 3¾" x 6", tan, black, and reddish brown, $400.00+ each.

Bear bank, 3¾" x 6", aqua, $400.00+.

Rare black bear with brown features standing by leaning 9" vase, $2,000.00+. Figurine also in black without brown features.

Rare panda bear bank, 3½" x 5", $1,000.00+.

Rare toothpick holder with bear standing beside tree stump, 2¼" x 2¼", $2,000.00+.

Rare panda figurine, 3½" x 5", $800.00+.

Black bear bank, 3¼" x 5¾", $400.00+.

Figurine bears, 3½" x 6½", tan bear and black bear with brown features, $300.00 – 350.00 each. Black bear with brown features and brown bear, 3¼" x 5¾", $300.00 – 350.00 each. Also in wine, bronze, black, or aqua.

Bear bookends, 3¾" x 6": brown single, $250.00 – 300.00, four pairs of black with brown features, tan, black, and reddish brown, $600.00+ pair. These bookends were made in "rights and lefts."

Bear pin, 2¾", $1,000.00+.

Bear cub salt/pepper shakers, 3½" male, 3" female, brown, light tan, tan, black with brown features, $60.00 – 75.00 pair. Two females can be a pair if one has three holes and the other has four holes. Two males can also be a pair if one has three holes and the other has four holes.

Bear cub figurines in black with brown features and reddish brown, male 3¼" x 2½", female 2¾" x 2", $75.00 – 100.00 each. Also in black or tan.

Bear pin, 2½", $1,000.00+.

Miniature figurine bears in various poses, two standing 1¾" x 2¼", $50.00 – 75.00 pair, 1¼" x 1¾" lying with leg up and 1¼" x 2¼" lying down, $50.00 – 75.00 pair. The two standing bears were also made in salt and pepper shakers.

LEFT:
Solid harnessed bears, 2¾" x 2½", renditions of a circus wrestling bear which came to Wahpeton, $300.00 – 350.00 each.

RIGHT:
Solid bear with "N. D. Rosemeade" mark, 2¾" x 2½", $300.00 – 350.00.

Bear cub 1¾" x 2¼" figurine on 5" ashtray, $200.00 – 250.00. Also advertising "Sheridan Wyoming – Heart of the Bighorn Mountains" or "GRAND MARAIS NORTH SHORE TREASURE CHEST."

1¼" x 2¼" bear figurine with brown features on 5" ashtray, $200.00 – 250.00.

Koala bear on tree trunk, 8½" x 3½", $250.00 – 300.00; koala bear on log planter, 5¼" x 5¼", $125.00 – 150.00.

Koala bear mother and cub figurines, 5½" x 3½", in white gloss and tan matt, $275.00 – 300.00 each.

PRODUCT LINES

Insects

Only a few insect motifs appear on Rosemeade pottery. While the butterflies symbolize the beauty of the prairie, the bees denote an important state agricultural product.

Bumble bee pins, 1¼", white and green, $300.00+ each. Also in aqua.

Covered box with bumble bee finial, 3¼" x 3½", $150.00 – 200.00. Also in green.

Butterfly design: 3½" creamer and 3" sugar, $50.00 – 75.00 set, Also in white, robin's egg blue, or light green. Two-compartment relish dish, 9" x 5½", $50.00 – 75.00 each. Also in white, robin's egg blue, or light green.

Theodore Roosevelt

Theodore Roosevelt National Park, the only national park in North Dakota and its foremost tourist attraction, inspired several Rosemeade commemoratives. American Guild writers described the Park Badlands as "one of the most extraordinary topographies on the surface of the earth, 110 square miles of breathtaking vistas."[1]

First coming to North Dakota in 1883 to hunt, Theodore Roosevelt soon became a rancher, acquiring the Maltese Cross Ranch near Medora. "A certain breed of person is beckoned, as was Theodore Roosevelt, by the singular challenge of a rugged, spirited land."[2]

Although Theodore Roosevelt only spent a short time in the North Dakota Badlands, "This wild and broken land had a profound impression on a young T.R."[3] Roosevelt once remarked, "I never would have been President if it had not been for my experience in North Dakota."[4] At the dawn of the twentieth century in 1901, Theodore Roosevelt became this nation's 26th President and one of its greatest conservationists. Theodore Roosevelt founded the U.S. Forest Service, signed the National Monuments Act, and established the first federal game preserve. His efforts led to the founding of the National Park Service.

North Dakotans are rightfully proud of Theodore Roosevelt. "The entire state unabashedly works T.R.'s name and face into its promotions."[5]

A Rosemeade teddy bear figurine appears alone and on ashtrays. The teddy bear was named for Theodore Roosevelt, who hunted and enjoyed observing bears in the wild. A famous political cartoon by Clifford Berryman portrayed Roosevelt and a bear cub, sparking an idea for a stuffed animal, "Teddy's bear."[6]

National Memorial Park plate, green, 8½" diameter, $350.00 – 375.00. Also in brown.

Postcard showing Theodore Roosevelt's ranch, which later became Roosevelt National Park.

3" Memorial Park mug with THEODORE ROOSEVELT MEMORIAL PARK and Maltese Cross (ranch brand) on one side and calf motif on back, $125.00 – 150.00.

5¾" Memorial Park pitcher, BADLANDS NORTH DAKOTA on back, $125.00 – 175.00.

Maltese Cross Ranch Cabin, original log cabin of Theodore Roosevelt during his ranching days in North Dakota. Banks, 2" x 3½", $350.00 – 400.00.

5" Park Trading Post ashtray, $125.00 – 150.00.

Extremely rare miniature log cabin, ¾" high x ¾" wide x 1½" long. The plastic mold, from Perma-Flex Cold Molding, Columbus, Ohio, used for this piece is on display at the Richland County Historical Museum.

Maltese Cross log cabin incense burner, 2" x 3½", $400.00 – 450.00. These Rosemeade authentic cabin copies also found an eager California market. They were sold as '49ers cabins on the centennial of the gold rush, promoted as incense burners or ashtrays.

Roosevelt head 3" mug, $175.00 – 225.00.

LEFT: Rare 8½" brown plate with Roosevelt ranch brands and nickname "Old-Four-Eyes," $1,000.00+. "While he was never classed as an expert cowhand, Roosevelt earned the respect of his peers, who eventually dropped the nickname, 'Old-Four-Eyes,' and referred to Roosevelt as 'fearless and a good rider.' "[7] RIGHT: Rare "OLD-FOUR-EYES" plate in green, $1,000.00+.

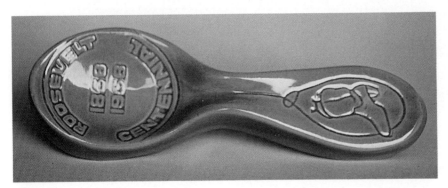

Centennial spoon rest, 8¾", $125.00 – 150.00.

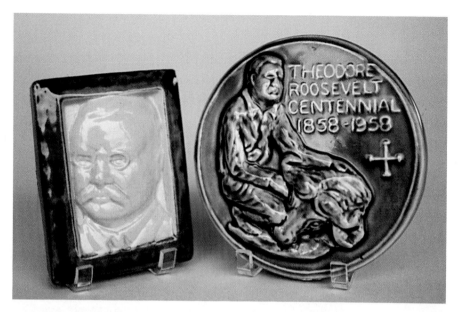

Roosevelt paperweight, 2¼" x 3", also in brown, $150.00 – 200.00. Centennial plate, 3¾", also in maroon, $150.00 – 175.00.

Teddy bear paperweight, 3½", $300.00 – 350.00.

Memorial Park 5" tray with teddy bear figurine, $350.00 – 400.00.

Place Souvenirs

Derived from the French word for memory, a souvenir serves as a memento or token of remembrance for a place. Local history buffs and collectors seek place souvenirs, such as Rosemeade ware.

International Peace Garden cairn: 3¾" paperweights, gray and tan, $125.00 – 150.00 each; 1¾" salt/pepper shakers, $150.00 – 175.00 pair; 4½" ashtray, U.S.A. on one side and CANADA on other side with gray cairn in center, $200.00 – 250.00 each.

Cairn at International Peace Garden, North Dakota-Manitoba Border

TO GOD IN HIS GLORY WE TWO NATIONS DEDICATE THIS GARDEN AND PLEDGE OURSELVES THAT AS LONG AS MEN LIVE WE WILL NOT TAKE UP ARMS AGAINST ONE ANOTHER

"Cairn at International Peace Garden" near Bottineau, North Dakota, postcard. Rosemeade paperweights, salt and pepper shakers, and ashtrays display "The Cairn," a mound of native stones erected as a landmark near the Peace Garden entrance. A stone tablet mounted on the cairn reads, "To God in His Glory...we two nations dedicate this garden and pledge ourselves that as long as man shall live, we will not take up arms against one another."

Postcard showing obelisk marking the approximate spot of the Geographical Center of North America at Rugby, North Dakota. An obelisk is "a tall, four sided shaft of stone usually tapering, that rises to a pyramidal point."[1] According to The World Almanac, "There is no generally accepted definition of geographic center and there is no satisfactory method for determining it. The geographic center of an area may be defined as the center of gravity of the surface... No marked or monumented point has been established by any government agency as the geographic center of either the fifty states, the conterminous U.S. or the North American continent. A monument was erected in Lebanon, Kansas, the conterminous U.S. center, by a group of citizens. A cairn in Rugby, North Dakota, marks the center of the North American continent."[2]

4¼" Geographical Center obelisk salt/pepper shakers, with four holes and two holes, $250.00+ pair. Also in gray.

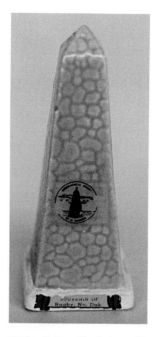

Single 4¼" salt shaker with "GEOGRAPHICAL CENTER OF NO. AMERICA" seal, $125.00 – 150.00.

4¾" Geographical Center of North Dakota obelisk figurines, made of white clay, clear glaze, and with no holes punched out and no plaques, $200.00+ each. (A sandy clay obelisk figurine with marbleized surface is pictured on page 36.)

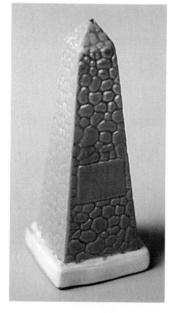

4¼" Geographical Center obelisk figurine with one hole at top to display a metal symbol like that at the top of the actual obelisk in Rugby, N.D., $200.00+.

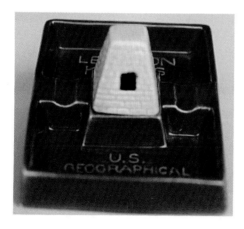

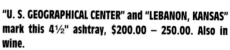

Photograph showing bottoms of sandy clay and white clay obelisks.

"U. S. GEOGRAPHICAL CENTER" and "LEBANON, KANSAS" mark this 4½" ashtray, $200.00 – 250.00. Also in wine.

Fort Abercrombie blockhouse on 5" ashtray, $300.00 – 350.00. Fort Abercrombie, 15 miles north of Wahpeton on the Red River, was established in 1858 by Colonel John J. Abercrombie as the first permanent U. S. military fort in North Dakota. During the Dakota Conflict of 1862, the fort was besieged by Sioux Warriors for almost six weeks. "Located where the West began in those days,"[3] Fort Abercrombie "served to guard wagon trains and steamboat traffic on the Red River, as a supply base for wagon trains headed to the Montana border and terminus for several major transportation routes throughout the northern plains."[4]

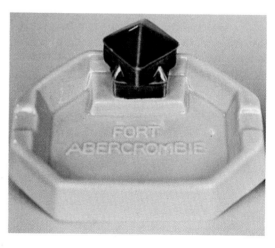

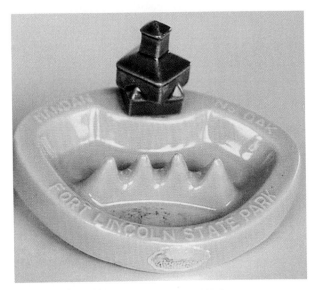

Rare Fort Lincoln State Park blockhouse with steeple, 1¾" salt/pepper shakers, $750.00+ pair. Fort Abercrombie blockhouse without steeple, 1" figurine, $200.00 – 250.00 each.

Fort Lincoln blockhouse on 5" ashtray, $300.00 – 350.00. Fort Abraham Lincoln located near Mandan, North Dakota, an important military post, was the headquarters for Lieutenant Colonel George Armstrong Custer and his Seventh Cavalry. In 1876, they rode out from this fort to their ill-fated encounter against the Sioux along the Little Bighorn River in eastern Montana. A look-out tower at the top of the blockhouse provided a wide overlook of the Missouri.

Rare Fort Abercrombie blockhouse salt/pepper shakers, 1¼", $750.00+ pair.

Bois De Sioux Golf Club plate, 6¾", $200.00 – 250.00. Land was contributed by Robert Hughes for this golf course located in two states, with part in Wahpeton, North Dakota, and the other part Breckenridge, Minnesota.

Garden Spot 6¾" plate, $250.00 – 300.00. Also in solid green.

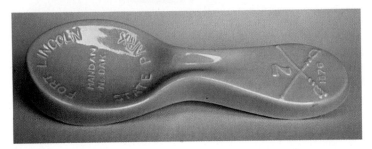

Fort Lincoln State Park spoon rest, 8¾", $100.00 – 125.00.

Rare Mount Rushmore figurine, 3⅝" x 5", bluish details on gray background, $500.00+.

God of Peace salt/pepper shakers: 6¾" pink, $500.00+ pair; 4" gold, $250.00 – 300.00 pair. Also in wine.

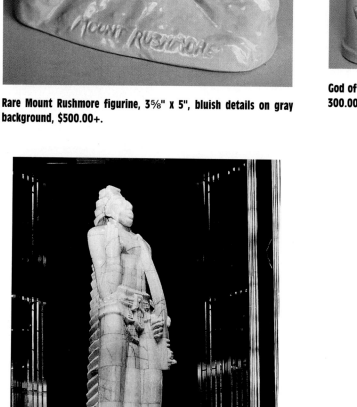

St. Paul, Minnesota is the home of the "Indian God of Peace," a 60-ton, 44' tall statue. Made of white Mexican onyx and designed by Carl Miles, the statue stands in the Veterans Memorial concourse of the City Hall and Courthouse building. The name was recently changed to "Vision of Peace."

Back of gold salt/pepper shakers.

Raised gold God of Peace plaque, 3¾" x 4¼", $100.00 – 125.00; green plaque, 3¾" x 4¼", $100.00 – 125.00.

Rare 8" maroon God of Peace vase, $500.00+.

Back of 8" vase.

God of Peace statues: 8¼" with 2¾" square base, $250.00 – 300.00; 7½" with 2" square base, $250.00 – 300.00.

God of Peace ashtray, 9½", $500.00+. Also in pink.

Rare 8¼" maroon plaque with "INDIAN GOD OF PEACE ST. PAUL MINNESOTA" on back, $500.00+. Also in green.

Centennials

Collectors and historians alike are interested in centennial souvenirs. Rosemeade pottery immortalized both state and city centennials in clay.

Button pin with Dakota Territory Centennial logo.

Dakota Territory Centennial white clay 7" square ashtray with decal, $75.00 – 125.00, ashtray made by Rosemeade Potteries.

4" Dakota Centennial plaque, $75.00 – 100.00.

Dakota Centennial white clay 5" square ashtray with decal, $100.00 – 150.00, ashtray made by Rosemeade Potteries.

LEFT:
7¼" Dakota Centennial plate with decal, $50.00 – 75.00.

RIGHT:
6" plaque with Dakota Centennial decal, $75.00 – 100.00.

7" Dakota Territory Centennial white clay ashtray with decal showing Sunny Nodak, state symbol (page 145), and advertising the *Fargo Forum* newspaper, $150.00 – 200.00. Ashtray made by Rosemeade Potteries, according to Joe McLaughlin.

7" Dakota Territory Centennial white clay ashtray with Sunny Nodak decal, promoting the state's Chamber of Commerce, GNDA, Greater North Dakota Association, $150.00 – 200.00. Ashtray made by Rosemeade Potteries.

Minnesota Centennial memorabilia: 3" mugs in brown, light green, and pink, $75.00 – 100.00 each; 7" jug, $125.00 – 175.00; 8" dark green spoon rest, $75.00 – 100.00. The pieces display Minnesota symbols, like Norway pine and ladyslipper.

Minnesota Centennial plaque, 7¼" x 7¾", $125.00 – 150.00.

Mark on Minnesota Centennial mug.

Minnesota Centennial plaque, 4½" x 3¾" $75.00 – 100.00.

LEFT:
Minnesota Centennial paperweight, 3¾", $125.00 – 150.00.

RIGHT:
Breckenridge, Minnesota, centennial plate, 6¾", $200.00 – 225.00.

Breckenridge Centennial reddish plaque, 4¼", $75.00 – 100.00. Also in blue. Green plaque with state shape raised instead of indented, 2¾", $75.00 – 100.00.

Breckenridge ashtray, 5", $175.00 – 200.00.

Aquarium

Records at the Richland County Historical Museum document the Wahpeton Pottery Company's production of several types of "Ornaments for Aquariums or Flower Bowls." Pieces described on a company stock listing were made of unglazed clay.

Although most aquarium items were unglazed, the twin turreted castle was made in both green gloss and brown gloss glaze. Another double castle was described in company literature as "bisque with red roofs and green grass." Because these articles turn a darker red when out in water, some unglazed examples may vary in color.

The Auburndale Goldfish Company in Chicago was a major purchaser, ordering 50 mermaids or 300 castles at a time in 1947 through 1950. However, by July of 1951, a letter from the Goldfish Company indicated that the castles were no longer selling well. In 1947, wholesale prices for castles, mermaids, and small coral were 35 cents each, with large coral, twin turreted castle, and Father Neptune 75 cents each. By 1950, wholesale prices had dropped to 15 cents each for castles, small coral, and mermaids and to 30 cents for Father Neptune.

Why did the aquarium marketing effort fail? Rosemeade's aquarium ware was mostly unglazed, contrary to other company product lines. Therefore, the Wahpeton Pottery Company was unable to compete with cheaper Japanese aquarium pieces, which looked similar.

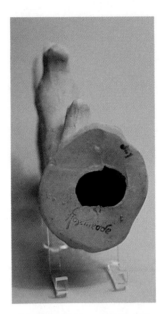

Extremely rare 6" unglazed large coral figurine, marked with ink stamp "Rosemeade" and the letter and number "J-1." Mark on base of large coral shown on right.

This extremely rare 4" unglazed goldfish bowl castle with ink stamp letter and number "J-4" on base has eight windows.

6" marked large coral shown with 4½" small coral. Both are extremely rare. Company information designated the small unglazed coral as "J-2."

Two extremely rare 3¾" unglazed castles. The castle on the right listed as "J-3" with four windows.

Extremely rare unglazed figurines: 3" x 4½" mermaid with holes in mouth and tail, "J-9"; 5½" x 6½" Father Neptune; 4½" x 3¾" upright mermaid with hole in mouth, "J-10"; 3" x 4¼" mermaid without holes in mouth and tail. Father Neptune, "J-8", came with a water jar. "A water plant may be grown in the jar which Father Neptune holds," according to the company stock listing. Another figurine, listed on an order form as "Twins," has not surfaced.

Extremely rare twin turreted castle, 4¾" x 5", unglazed item, lettered and numbered "J-5."

Extremely rare twin turreted castle with green gloss glaze, 4¾" x 5". Also in brown gloss glaze.

Egyptian Design

"Modern styling and historic design are combined"[1] in usable ware for the Egyptian Design line. Laura Taylor Hughes was fascinated with Egyptian pottery. She owned several examples and kept a large file of clippings for inspiration.

Egyptian design: 5" x 5½" antique gray jardinieres with black base. "The dark waters of the River Nile make a decorative base," showing scenes of both sides, "fish and wild ducks swimming among lotus flowers,"[2] between traditional Egyptian borders, with green gloss planter and porous bisque planter to fit inside jardinieres. Jardiniere and planter, $250.00 – 300.00 set. Also in antique green.

Four canopic jars, 3¼" to 3½", "fitted with corks, used for either salt and pepper or spices," $600.00+ set of four. "Modeled from the canopic jars of Ancient Egypt..., the lids [with one to four holes] are carved to represent the four genii [guardian spirits] of Egyptian Hades, who, according to Egyptian mythology preside over the four points of the compass."[3] The jars were boxed in sets of four with an accompanying story "which tells something of the history and use of the original canopic jars." The jars were made in antique gray and antique green, the antique effect created by rubbing the piece with charcoal dust after the first firing. Backs of four canopic jars shown below.

5" x 5½" Egyptian design jardiniere in green gloss glaze, fish motif on one side, wild ducks on the other side, $200.00 – 250.00.

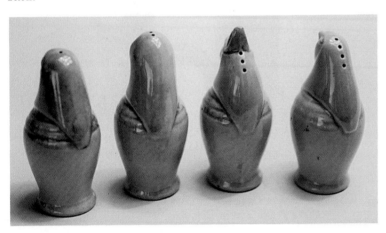

8" Egyptian design vase with motif of youth playing stringed instrument, $200.00 – 250.00. Also in antique gray.

5½" Egyptian wall vases "from ancient Egypt, land of lotus flowers and romance" in complementary scenes. The first vase shows "a dainty maid plucks a lotus blossom" and the second vase, "while a dark-skinned youth with his stringed instrument serenades her with a song."[4] The porous bisque planter is shown in the center. The vases were made in "antique glazed finish in gray or green with black base." Vase with planter, $250.00 – 300.00; vase without planter, $200.00 – 250.00. Also in antique green.

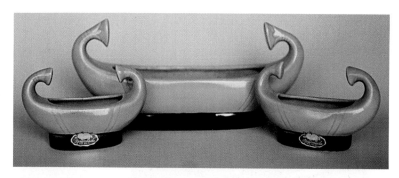

Egyptian boats: 4½" x 9½" flower bowl with two 3" x 4¾" candleholders, $300.00 – 350.00 set. Also in blue with blue base or black with black base.

Egyptian boat single candleholders, 3" x 4¾", black and blue, $50.00 – 75.00 each.

5½" Egyptian wall vase in light blue gloss glaze, $200.00 – 250.00.

Human Forms

In contrast to many other potteries of that era, the Wahpeton Pottery Company and later Rosemeade Potteries produced only a limited number of human form designs. Others are pictured in the Native American, Egyptian, and Centennials sections.

Extremely rare decal of Christ on 6⅛" tile. Made for a southern company, according to Joe McLaughlin.

Extremely rare chef salt/pepper shakers, 3¼".

Extremely rare 3¼" chef figurine on 7" black ashtray, "Good-foodfully Yours – Chef Louie's" made for a Mitchell, South Dakota restaurant.

Paul Bunyan and Babe the Blue Ox salt/pepper shakers, 2¼", $125.00 – 150.00 pair. Mythical Paul Bunyan, lumberjack of superhuman size and strength, was one of Laura Taylor's few shakers featuring people. Tall tales of his extraordinary feats echoed through the camps of white pine lumbermen, especially during the late 1800s and early 1900s logging boom. Laura Taylor stated in her 1950 correspondence that she was designing "a salt and pepper set featuring Paul Bunyan and Babe, the Blue Ox, for Bemidji, Minnesota."[1] Since the late 1930s, many northern Minnesota towns had lured tourists with Paul Bunyan and Babe attractions, museums, parks, and large concrete statues. After loaning Hughes figurines of Paul Bunyan and Ox to study, C. W. Richards of the Bemidji Beltrami Hardware store became the exclusive distributor in the area. Successful sales to tourists accelerated Paul and Babe to "number one on the hit parade for 1950."[2]

Extremely rare 3¼" chef figurine on 7" green ashtray, "Good-foodfully Yours – Chef Louie's" made for a Mitchell, South Dakota restaurant.

University of North Dakota Norwegian girl figurine, 4¾", costumed similarly to the Rosemeade version. Made for Prince Olaf and Crown Princess Martha when they visited UND in 1939.

Aztec Indian 2" pin, $1,000.00+.

Extremely rare 3" girl and 3¼" boy, "ANNE K Wahpeton, N.D." black ink stamp and incised "AK" mark. Girl and boy figurines in Norwegian costume, made as banquet centerpiece for royalty visiting Wahpeton.

Rare Sunny Nodak mug, 4¾", $250.00 – 300.00 Sunny Nodak appears on several Rosemeade items. In 1957, Sunny Nodak became the symbol for the Greater North Dakota Association. Within six months, "the enthusiastic character, symbolic of pleasant living in North Dakota, has met with favorable response over all of North Dakota and much of the entire nation."[3] Business firms were encouraged to "use Sunny Nodak to promote not only their business, but also the great state of North Dakota."[4]

Rare King Pin Foods salt/pepper shakers, 4¼", $400.00+ pair. Although these salt and pepper shakers are unmarked, Laura Taylor's drawing of the figure documents her production design and pairs have been seen in private collections.

7" x 2½" maid with horn planter, $150.00 – 200.00. Also in blue.

Mermaid planter, 4¾" x 3¾", $200.00 – 250.00.

Rare maid in crescent moon wall pocket, 6½", $500.00+.

Cowboy ashtray, 4½", $100.00 – 125.00.

Harold's Cafe ashtray with western motif, 4¾", $125.00 – 150.00. Also for QUEEN CITY – DICKINSON – NORTH DAKOTA. The cowboy design was created by Rosemeade employee Emma Althoff.

Native American

Sitting Bull, the great Hunkpapa Sioux leader, was recognized in Laura Taylor's designs. The State Historical Society of North Dakota describes the chief as "an inspired leader of his people during an extremely difficult era of conflict between the American military and the native peoples of the northern plains."[1] Well known for his decisive victory over Custer at The Battle of the Little Bighorn, people were fascinated by Sitting Bull. An eloquent speaker with great love for his people and native earth, Sitting Bull toured with Buffalo Bill Cody's Wild West Show.

Museum papers indicate that the Wahpeton High School annual photo of Joseph Brant, a Native American boy from South Dakota, was used for some Rosemeade ashtrays. "The Wahpeton Pottery in looking for a typically Indian picture to use on pottery chose the one of Joseph Brant. It was modeled in low relief by Laura Taylor and will be used on various items whenever an Indian head is needed."[2]

Chief Sitting Bull: 3½" mug with handle, $250.00 – 300.00; 2⅝" salt/pepper shakers, $500.00+ pair; 3½" mug without handle, $250.00 – 300.00.

5¼" Native American plate, made by Laura Taylor at UND.

Back of Sitting Bull mug, showing correct date of treaty. The Laramie Treaty of the Western Sioux, Sitting Bull's territory, was signed in 1868. There was a treaty signed with the Eastern Sioux, not involving Sitting Bull, in 1867. Since this mug depicts Sitting Bull, former Rosemeade employee Olga Hecktner stated the date was incorrect and should have been 1868.

Arrowhead "SITTING BULL" ashtrays, 5¼", gray and wine, $125.00 – 150.00 each. Also in green or brown. Made in 1953 as town souvenirs for North and South Dakota. The "first shipment went to Mobridge, South Dakota where his bones rest," according to papers of Laura Taylor.

Wigwam, or teepee, shelter for plains Native American tribes, 2¾" incense burner with 1¾" bisque incense holder, $300.00 – 350.00.

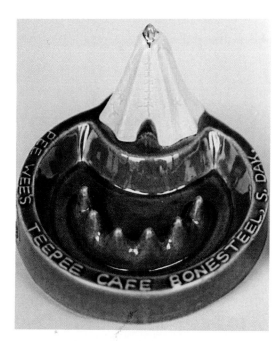

5½" teepee ashtray incised mark on bottom "Chahinkapa No. Dak." for sale at the Chahinkapa Park in Wahpeton, $150.00 – 175.00. Also in green.

5½" ashtray with Native American motif, $150.00 – 175.00.

5" teepee figurine ashtray, advertising "TEEPEE CAFE," $250.00 – 275.00.

Native American ashtray, 4¼", $150.00 – 175.00. Also in green or pink.

Accessories

History abounds with a long sentimental fascination for shoes. Puss-n-Boots, The Old Woman in the Shoe, Cinderella and the glass slipper, and Dorothy and her red shoes are loved children's stories. From the old shoes tied to a honeymoon car for good luck to religious practices and the Native American admonition to "never judge a man until you have walked a day in his moccasins," shoes permeate our culture. Shoes have been collected since first made as small objects in the seventeenth century with increasing popularity in Victorian England, followed by American interest. Rosemeade joined many other potteries who made products in the form of shoes, boots, and hats.

Rare Red Wing Shoes company advertising items: pen holder with 4¼" square tile and 2¼" Irish setter boot, $650.00+; 4¾" mug, $850.00+; 7" ashtray with 2¾" Irish setter boot, $1,200.00+.

Rare Irish setter boot figurine, 2¾" x 2½", $500.00+.

Wooden shoe planters, 2¾" x 5¾", rose, aqua, and blue, $45.00 – 65.00 each. Also in gold or wine.

Ladies button slippers, 2¼" x 4½", light blue, rose gold, creme, black, aqua, $45.00 – 65.00 each. Also in wine.

Wooden shoe planter with floral design, 2¾" x 5¼", $85.00 – 100.00.

Bisque miniature shoes with hand-painted designs, 1½" x 3½", advertised as "Indian moccasins," $50.00 – 65.00 each.

Bisque miniature wooden shoes with tulip decoration in pink and blue, 1¼" x 2½", $85.00 – 100.00 each.

Ranger boots: 4" x 2¾" rose and aqua, $50.00 – 65.00; 7" x 4¾" aqua, $50.00 – 65.00. Also in black and bronze, molded from worn old boots.

Rare pair of women's western boots with different shapes for right and left feet, 5¼" x 3½", $200.00 – 250.00. Also in black or bronze. Rosemeade, along with many other pottery companies, produced cowboy boots. Each characteristic feature of this highly distinctive shoe had a purpose. The high boot protected the cowboy's legs from the rough brush. While the pointed toe facilitated finding the stirrup easily, the high heel kept the rider's foot from slipping through the stirrup. Decorative stitching stiffened the leather, preventing curling at the top and wrinkling at the ankle.

LEFT:
Miniature cowboy boot figurine, 2" x 1¾", $75.00 – 100.00.

RIGHT:
Cowboy boot figurine on 5" ashtray, $150.00 – 200.00. Also advertising "Cowboy Capital Boothill Dodge City, Kansas."

Cowboy hat advertising ashtrays, 1¾" x 3", $75.00 – 100.00 each. Also in black and with advertisement for "CUSTER, S.D.," "BADLANDS, S.D.," "SANISH, N.D.," and "THE OUTLAW, WINNER, S.D." Cowboy hats were another popular product of many potteries. Considered a necessity, cowboy hats varied from region to region, but all assumed "a basic form that set them apart from the headgear worn by non-cowpokes."[1] With the high crown providing insulation from the hot sun, the wide rim functioned as a sunshade and sometimes as an umbrella.

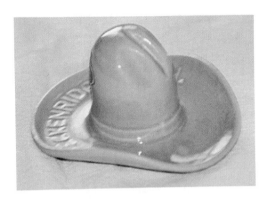

Cowboy hat advertising ashtray, 1¾" x 3", $75.00 – 100.00.

2½" x 5" hand-thrown sombrero. Sometimes demonstrated on the potter's wheel for groups like Rotary International, $150.00 – 200.00.

Functional

"It is in producing objects of household service that clay is found at its best."[1] Shapes of functional pieces have shown little variation over centuries of time, with simpler forms being of more practical usage. In the fifties, as functionality became the emphasis of many pottery manufacturers, Rosemeade potteries produced an extensive array of useful pottery.

Windmill salt/pepper shakers "with plastic fans" and metal fasteners, 3½", $150.00 – 200.00 pair. Also in wine.

Sailboat salt/pepper shakers, 3½" x 3¾", some marked with city names and others plain, $400.00+ pair. This sailboat shape was also popular with other potteries of the time, especially California potteries. A larger similarly shaped sailboat figurine, made in Czechoslovakia, is on display as part of Laura Taylor's collection at the Richland County Historical Museum.

2¾" rounded ball salt/pepper shakers, $75.00 – 125.00 pair. Also in tan or aqua.

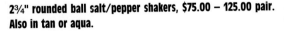

Grain shock-shaped salt/pepper shakers, 4¾", $125.00 – 150.00 pair. Also in green, brown, or yellow.

Salt/pepper shakers of two rounded balls, 4½", $75.00 – 125.00 pair.

4¾" salt/pepper shakers, $75.00 – 125.00 pair.

Hand-thrown bowl, 3¼" x 8¾", signature piece with "F. Lantz" on bottom, $150.00 – 175.00. The fluted edges were made by squeezing the rim between thumb and forefinger like on a pie crust.

Hand-thrown bowl, 1¾" x 6¼", signed "F. Lantz" on bottom, $125.00 – 150.00.

Hand-thrown bowl, 2" x 11¼", inscribed "F. Lantz" with "NORTH DAKOTA Rosemeade" blue ink stamp on bottom, $125.00 – 150.00.

PRODUCT LINES

Hand-thrown fluted rim bowl, 3" x 7", signed "F. Lantz" on bottom, $125.00 – 150.00; plain edge bowl, 2" x 6¼", $75.00 – 100.00.

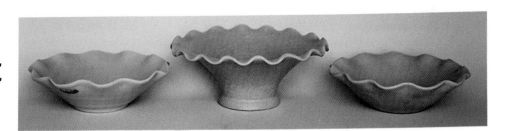

Bowls with fluted rims: 2" x 10½" bowl, 4¼" x 10½" bowl, 2½" x 11¼" bowl, $75.00 – 100.00 each.

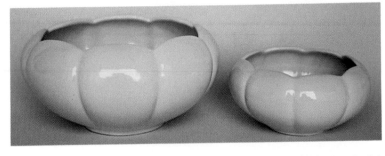

3½" x 7" flower bowl and 2¼" x 5" candy dish, $35.00 – 50.00 each. Also in pale pink, black, light green, or dark green.

Hand-thrown bowl, 1¾" x 6½", shaded pink to blue at fluted rim, $150.00 – 200.00.

Hand-thrown bowl, 2" x 4½", shaded pink to blue, $75.00 – 100.00.

Hand-thrown bowl, 1½" x 4¼", with "Rosemeade NO. DAK." mark, $75.00 – 100.00.

Bronze bowl, 3" x 5¼", $50.00 – 75.00.

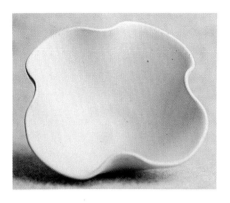

Hand-thrown bowl with four indentions, 2" x 4½", $50.00 – 75.00.

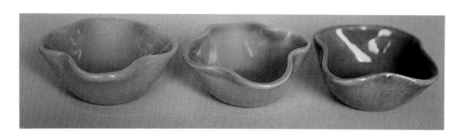

2¼" nut cups, blue, strawberry, and lilac, $20.00 – 35.00 each. Also in walnut brown or moss green.

Hand-thrown bowl with three indentions, 2¼" x 4", $50.00 – 75.00.

Hand-thrown bowl with blue/black crackle glaze, 2¼" x 5", $75.00 – 100.00

The cloverleaf bowl came in two sizes, 5" and 3½", $35.00 – 50.00 each. Also in walnut brown, strawberry, moss green, or blue.

Fluted hand-thrown vase, 3¾", $50.00 – 75.00.

2¼" creamer and 2" sugar, $50.00 – 75.00 set; 3" x 8" fluted basket, $45.00 – 65.00; 4½" fluted vase, $35.00 – 50.00. The fluted vase was also made in a 6¼" size. Also in walnut brown, strawberry, moss green, blue, or black.

Round 7½" bowl, $50.00 – 75.00. Also in walnut brown, strawberry, moss green, or blue. 1½" x 3" flower holder, $10.00 – 25.00. Also in moss green, black, walnut brown, strawberry, or blue, and with 3½" fluted candleholders.

2½" barrels, possibly toothpick holders, $75.00 – 100.00 each.

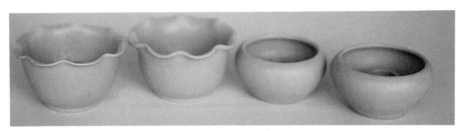

Candleholders: 2" x 3¾" fluted, $75.00 – 100.00 pair; 1½" x 3" plain, $50.00 – 75.00 pair.

5¼" candleholders, $100.00 – 125.00 pair.

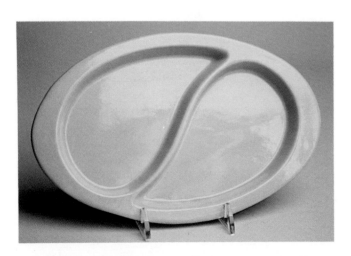

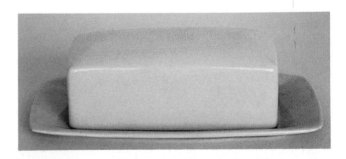

Butter dish for ¼-pound butter, 2¼" x 5½" cover and 3½" x 7¾" tray, $125.00 – 150.00. Also in cream white, ice blue, sprout green, or with rooster pattern.

Two-compartment relish dish, 9" x 5½", $50.00 – 75.00. Also in robin's egg blue, lime green, or ivory white.

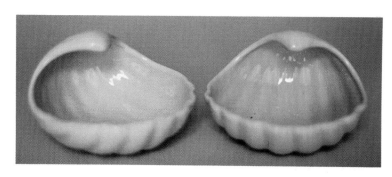

7¼" hand-thrown plate, shaded green to black, $150.00 – 175.00.

Rare 2" hand-thrown cup with 4½" hand-thrown saucer, $200.00 – 250.00. Chinese tea bowls were the first tea holders. After explorers brought tea to Europe during the 16th century, "the English chose to drink their tea hot whereas the Chinese had drunk it barely warm. This fact made it necessary for the English to add a handle and later a saucer to their tea bowls and so the tea cup and saucer set was born."[2] Although cups were part of various lunch sets, Rosemeade cup and saucer sets are scarce.

2¼" hand-thrown cup with twisted handle, $75.00 – 100.00.

3" mustache cup, $100.00 – 150.00. Also in maroon, lime green, or pink. Invention of the mustache cup is credited to the Staffordshire Pottery of Harvey Adams. To prevent wet whiskers while drinking tea, a small ledge was added near the cup rim. As the mustache rested on this ledge and remained dry, liquid flowed through the opening between the ledge and side of the cup.

Shell candy dishes, 2¾" x 4½", in cream white with ice blue and cream white with light green lining, $50.00 – 75.00 each. Also in cream white with pink lining.

Plain 4¼" mug, $100.00 – 125.00. Mugs, resembling tankards but smaller and without lids, have been used as drinking vessels since the 1700s. They were easier to make than cups.

Extremely rare Harvest Gold glaze 4" tumbler.

Extremely rare Mirror Blue glaze 4" tumbler.

Hand-thrown vase with fluted rim, 6½", $75.00 – 100.00.

6¼" ridged vase, $75.00 – 100.00; 4½" vase with enlarged top, $50.00 – 75.00; 6¾" vase with three rings at top, $75.00 – 100.00.

Old western-style bath tub, 3½", $125.00 – 150.00. Rosemeade Potteries made this piece to resemble the bath tub in the Chateau de Mores, home of Marquis de Mores, a French aristocrat and ill-fated entrepreneur of the 1800s. The Chateau has been preserved as a State Historic Site near Medora, North Dakota.

Hand-thrown fluted rim vases: 5¾" blue, 5¾" blue, and 4½" pink, $75.00 – 100.00 each.

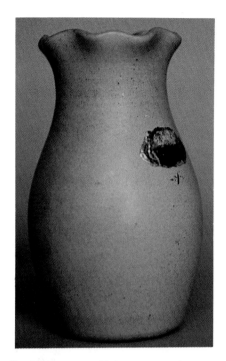

4½" hand-thrown vase, $75.00 – 100.00.

3¾" vase, made to look hand-thrown with ridge on the vase exterior, $50.00 – 75.00.

Hand-thrown vase with fluted rim, 4", $75.00 – 100.00.

Tan shaded to white vase, 5¼", $75.00 – 100.00; blue vase, 3½", $50.00 – 75.00; tan vase, 6½", $75.00 – 100.00.

Rare green vase with gunmetal drip glaze and interior, 7¾", $175.00 – 200.00.

LEFT:
6" hand-thrown vase with early Meadow Green glaze, marked "No. Dak. Rosemeade," $100.00 – 125.00.

RIGHT:
6¾" hand-thrown vase, marked "N. D. Rosemeade," $100.00 – 125.00.

Hand-thrown Harvest Gold vase, 4½", marked
"Rosemeade No. Dak." $150.00 – 175.00.

Black/blue crackle glaze vase, 5",
$75.00 – 100.00.

Hand-thrown aqua vase shaded
with rose matt glaze, 5¾", $75.00 –
100.00.

5" vase with unusual Chinese jade glaze, "Rosemeade No. Dak." mark, $100.00 – 125.00.

13½" vase with 7¾" container top and 5½"
base, $125.00 – 150.00.

7¾" vase, $75.00 – 100.00.

Vases: 2" black, 3" aqua, 4" green,
4½" tan, 4" blue low vase, 4"
maroon, 3¼" yellow, $50.00 – 75.00
each. All in other colors.

Bud vases: 7½" pale pink, $50.00 – 75.00; 6" aqua, $50.00 – 75.00; 5¾" pale pink, $50.00 – 75.00; 4¾" forest green, $20.00 – 30.00; 5½" tan, $35.00 – 50.00; 4¾" black, $20.00 – 30.00; 5½" yellow, $35.00 – 50.00; 4¾" lilac, $20.00 – 30.00; 5¾" yellow, $35.00 – 50.00; 7½" forest green, $50.00 – 75.00. The last bud vase on the right also made in pale pink, light blue, black, or light green. Others were also made in various colors.

Double vase with twisted handle, 9¼", $150.00 – 200.00.

Hand-thrown black/blue crackle glaze vase, 5", $150.00 – 200.00.

4½" vase with upturned rim, $50.00 – 75.00.

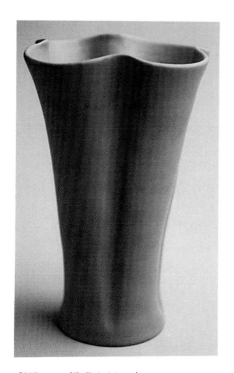

8¾" vase with fluted top, $100.00 – 125.00.

4½" x 7" fan vase, also in rose or ivory, $75.00 – 100.00. 5¾" fluted top vase, $75.00 – 100.00.

PRODUCT LINES

The Square Vase in three sizes: 10½" pink shaded with gray, $100.00 – 125.00; 9" white shaded with pink, $75.00 – 100.00; 7½" light green shaded with green, $75.00 – 100.00. Also in ivory shaded with green, forest green, or black.

Black and gold spattered glaze with gold interiors vases, 5" and 4", $100.00 – 125.00 each. Also in black and blue spattered glaze with blue interiors.

9" vase with squared sides, $100.00 – 125.00.

9" yellow vase, $75.00 – 100.00.

9¼" vase, $75.00 – 100.00. Also in black.

Ridged vases:
BACK ROW: 5¼" light blue, 5¼" tan, 6¾" green, 6" blue. FRONT ROW: 4¼" blue, 3½" light blue, $75.00 – 100.00 each.

5¾" vase, $75.00 – 100.00.

Pink ringed bowl, 4¼" x 5½", $75.00 – 100.00; lime green vase with rings at bottom, 6", $75.00 – 100.00.

4¾" vase with ridged top, $75.00 – 100.00.

Hand-thrown vase with black/blue crackle glaze, 5¼", $100.00 – 125.00.

Ridged vase, 6½", $75.00 – 100.00.

LEFT:
4" pitcher, $75.00 – 100.00.

RIGHT:
3¼" pitcher, $50.00 – 75.00.

8¾" pitcher and 9½" vase with bronze glaze, $100.00 – 125.00 each.

8½" orange pitcher, 12" brown vase, 9¼" yellow vase, $100.00 – 125.00 each.

Extremely rare 3½" hand-thrown pitcher with hand-applied double handle.

3½" pitcher with early blue/black glaze, $100.00 – 125.00.

3½" "CARRY A NATION" pitcher with her picture in front and "MEDICINE LODGE KANSAS" in back, commemorating the Temperance Movement and Carry Nation, who closed many saloons in Kansas, $100.00 – 125.00.

4" pitcher, advertised as "Syrup Jug," $75.00 – 125.00.

4½" pitcher with unusual handle, $100.00 – 125.00.

Pitchers: 3¼" tan, $25.00 – 35.00; 3¾" blue, $50.00 – 75.00; 5½" tan, $45.00 – 65.00.

Hand-thrown pitcher with applied handle, 3¼", $75.00 – 100.00.

2⅝" pitcher, $35.00 – 50.00.

5½" pitcher with Shrine organization symbol and words "GRAND LODGE No. DAK." on other side, $50.00 – 75.00.

3½" pitcher, $50.00 – 75.00.

Hand-thrown pinched handle pitcher, 2¾", $75.00 – 100.00.

1¼" miniature pitcher, $100.00 – 125.00.

Three pitchers with rings: 4" dark green gloss glaze, 3½" blue gloss, 3½" bronze, $100.00 – 125.00 each.

Pitchers: 4¼" lime green advertising "Gackle Jubilee June 8 – 9, 1954," also in pink, $50.00 – 75.00; 3¼" blue, $50.00 – 75.00; 3" white, $50.00 – 75.00; 3" reddish, $50.00 – 75.00; 3½" pink with advertising "ALFRED OLSON FAIRWAY STORE MILACA MINN.," $50.00 – 75.00.

Advertised as "Flower Pitcher," this 8" pitcher was described as Icelandic in Laura Taylor's drawing of the piece, $100.00 – 125.00.

Twisted handle pitchers: 5¼" brown, 5¼" blue, 4¼" blue, $100.00 – 125.00 each.

2¼" pitcher, $50.00 – 75.00.

2" miniature pitcher, $100.00 – 125.00.

Miniature 2" x 3" blue sugar bowl with handles and 2" x 1¾" creamer, also in black, pink, or green, $75.00 – 100.00 set; 3¾" x 4" pink creamer and 2½" x 4¼" sugar, $50.00 – 75.00 set; 3½" x 2½" bluish green creamer and 2½" x 3" sugar with lugs instead of handles, also in cream white, pale pink, or robin's egg blue, $50.00 – 75.00 set.

Hand-thrown 3¼" sugar and 3¼" creamer with hand-applied handle, $100.00 – 125.00 set. To make handmade handles, strips of clay are cut from a slab or "pulled" between the thumb and fingers, stretching to the desired size. After the clay becomes firm, the handle is brushed with slip to attach it to the piece.

Hand-thrown 2" sugar and 2¼" creamer, "NORTH DAKOTA Rosemeade" mark, $100.00 – 125.00 set.

3" sugar and 3" creamer, $50.00 – 75.00 set.

Hand-thrown 2½" creamer and 2½" sugar, "NORTH DAKOTA Rosemeade" mark, $100.00 – 125.00 set.

Sugar and creamer sets: blue 2½" x 2¾" sugar and 2½" x 3¾" creamer, $75.00 – 100.00 set; pink 2½" x 2¾" sugar and 2½" x 3" creamer, $75.00 – 100.00 set.

3" sugar and 3¾" creamer, $50.00 – 75.00 set. Also in pink.

Miniature twisted handle 2" sugar and 2" creamer, $200.00 – 225.00 set.

3" sugar and 3½" creamer for church celebration, $50.00 – 75.00. Also in white, robin's egg blue, or green.

Hand-thrown baskets with twisted handles applied by hand, 3" x 5" and 3¼" x 4½", "NORTH DAKOTA Rosemeade" mark, $125.00 – 150.00. In a Rotary International speech, Laura Taylor described making hand-thrown baskets with twisted handles.

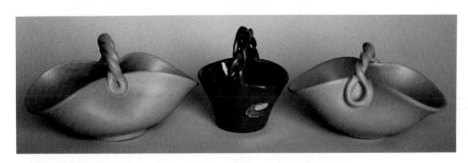

Baskets with twisted handles: 3" x 5¼" pink, 3" x 2¾" blue, 3" x 2¾" pink, $100.00 – 125.00 each.

Baskets: 2¾" x 3½" pink, $25.00 – 35.00; 4¼" x 4¾", $35.00 – 50.00.

3" pierced bowl for flowers, also in green or pink, $35.00 – 50.00; 1½" x 6¾" fluted bowl, $50.00 – 75.00; 2" blue container, possibly a toothpick holder, $50.00 – 75.00; 3" leaf design bowl shaded tan to peach, often called a rose bowl, also in pink or blue, $35.00 – 50.00.

Flower holders: 3½", 2¾", 2½", $50.00 – 75.00 each. Also in green.

Advertised as "Floral Spheres": 4½", 5", 5½", $35.00 – 50.00 each. Also in pink or blue.

Pitcher with flower holder holes, 5½" x 5½",
$75.00 – 100.00.

Called "Stump Flower Holders" by the company, these 2" x 3½" holders were
made in wine or green, $100.00 – 125.00 each.

4½" Floral Sphere with three rows of holes instead
of two rows, $35.00 – 50.00.

Cream white "Posy Rings," commonly known as pansy rings:
two 4½" rings, also in jet black, pale pink, moss green, or
robin's egg blue, $25.00 – 50.00 each; 8" ring, also in jet black,
pale pink, moss green, or robin's egg blue, $50.00 – 75.00.

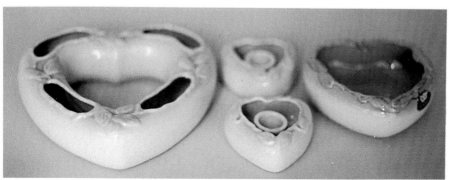

Heart-shaped items: 7" Posy Ring, $125.00 –
150.00; 3" candleholders, $100.00 – 125.00 pair;
5" flower bowl or candy dish, $100.00 – 125.00.

PRODUCT LINES

2½" x 6¼" planter, $50.00 – 75.00. Also in black and other colors.

3¾" x 5¼" planters, $50.00 – 75.00 each. Also in other colors.

7½" floral planters, $50.00 – 75.00 each. Also in shaded blue to purple.

Strawberry planter, 6" x 7¼", $200.00 – 225.00.

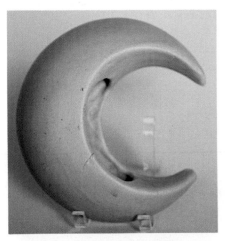

4¼" crescent moon wall pocket, $50.00 – 75.00.

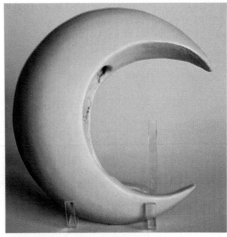

6¼" crescent moon wall pocket, advertised as "ideal for ivy," $250.00 – 300.00.

Green textured glaze created by Joe McLaughlin on 4" x 5½" flowerpot, $200.00 – 225.00.

6" x 7¼" strawberry planter, $200.00 – 225.00.

Two bronze flowerpots: 4¼" x 5¾" at left; 4" x 5½" at right with original 39¢ price on base, $200.00 – 225.00 each.

LEFT:
2¼" x 4½" cigarette box, $225.00 – 250.00. Also in yellow, blue, or pink.

RIGHT:
3" ashtray, $100.00 – 125.00. Although these ashtrays matched the 4½" cigarette box of same design, the ashtrays were sold separately.

Rare Viking ship planters: 4¾" x 10" robin's egg blue, $200.00 – 250.00; 5¼" x 12" light green, $200.00 – 250.00; 3¾" x 6" pale pink, $150.00 – 200.00. Also in dark green, ivory white, or aqua.

Viking ship figurine on 5" ashtray, $300.00 +.

Rare Viking ship salt/pepper shakers, 1½" x 3½", $400.00 – 450.00 pair. Also in white, green, or aqua.

Modern Design: 1½" salt/pepper shakers, $35.00 – 50.00 pair; 2" sugar and 2" creamer, $35.00 – 50.00 set. "This attractive modern set has both beauty and utility," an advertisement stated. Colors were listed as black, aqua, wine, rose, blue, or coral. Rosemeade's "Modern Design" followed a popular trend. For example, the Tiempo line introduced in 1949 by Gladding McBean of Los Angeles, California, was "notable for its 'modernistic' squared-off shape."[3]

Rare Modern Design 3¼" ashtray, $125.00 – 150.00. Also in black, aqua, wine, rose, or coral. Since the ashtray was soon discontinued, quantities were limited and the piece is scarce.

Advertising

Because advertising is such a part of our lives, many advertising pieces invoke nostalgia, and interest in advertising collectibles heightens. Trademarks or logos of products used throughout the years become beloved symbols.

Advertising give-aways have a long history in the United States since the Civil War. They have been used to reward customers and keep the company name on the market.

As was true of many potteries of the time, the Wahpeton Pottery Company and Rosemeade Potteries produced large quantities of advertising items, especially ashtrays. National parks, states, banks, golf courses, centennials, chicken feed, and oil and ice cream companies placed special orders. Laura Taylor's business card read "Custom Made Ceramics." Joe McLaughlin placed even more emphasis on advertising ware. Many Rosemeade ashtrays and other advertising pieces are shown in other sections of the book.

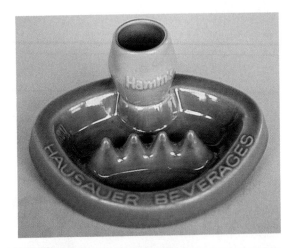

5" green ashtray advertising Hausauer Beverages, with Hamm's Beer gray barrel figurine, $500.00+.

3¼" Grain Belt salt shaker, made for Hausauer Beverages, $500.00+. Single shakers with one hole were made for beer distributors. Given as advertising promotions to their customers, the shakers were used in bars to salt beer.

5" brown ashtray advertising Hausauer Beverages, with Hamm's tan barrel figurine, $500.00+.

United States map tray, 6¾", $500.00+. Wyoming state map tray with state nickname, 5", $50.00 – 75.00. Called state map trays by the company, these items may be ashtrays or pin trays, depending on whether a notch is present.

Extremely rare large United States map tray, 5¼" x 7¾".

5¾" Iowa state map trays, maroon and green, $200.00 – 250.00 each.

State map trays: 5½" Alabama, 5¼" Mississippi, $50.00 – 75.00 each.

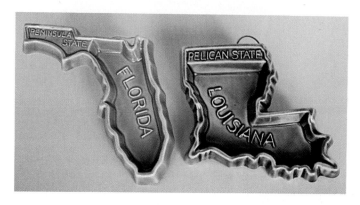

State map trays: 5" Florida, $125.00 – 150.00; 5" Louisiana, $100.00 – 125.00.

State map trays: 5¼" Indiana, $100.00 – 125.00; 4¼" Missouri, $75.00 – 100.00.

State map trays: 4¾" Wisconsin, $75.00 – 100.00; 5½" North Dakota, $50.00 – 75.00.

State map trays: 5¼" Illinois, $75.00 – 100.00; 5½" New York, $75.00 – 100.00.

State map trays: 5¾" Washington, $35.00 – 50.00; 5¾" Texas, $75.00 – 100.00.

State map trays: 5¼" Oregon, $35.00 – 50.00; 6½" Oklahoma, $50.00 – 75.00.

State map trays: 4¾" Minnesota, $50.00 – 75.00; 5½" Kansas, $50.00 – 75.00.

State map trays: 5¾" Montana, $50.00 – 75.00; 5½" South Dakota, $50.00 – 75.00.

State map trays: 4¾" Arkansas, $75.00 – 100.00; 4½" Georgia, $75.00 – 100.00.

State map trays: 6" Nebraska, $50.00 – 75.00; 8" Tennessee, $35.00 – 50.00.

State map trays: 6¼" Kentucky, $50.00 – 75.00; 5½" Pennsylvania, $50.00 – 75.00.

5¼" Vermont state map tray, $75.00 – 100.00.

4½" Ohio state map tray, $75.00 – 100.00.

Ashley, North Dakota Diamond Jubilee ashtray, 4¾", $75.00 – 100.00. This ashtray was made from white clay and the decals applied at Rosemeade Potteries, according to Joe McLaughlin. The ware was made in advance of the 1963 celebration as Rosemeade Potteries ceased production in 1961.

These state map trays were used for advertising, souvenirs, organizations, and so on. A few are shown and others listed as many different variations in several colors exist and others constantly surface.

5½" North Dakota state map tray made for anniversary of Kulm State Bank, $50.00 – 75.00.

5½" Kansas state map tray, souvenir of the Eisenhower Museum, $50.00 – 75.00.

Some of the other ashtrays with North Dakota map shape are Bismarck – First National Bank 75th Anniversary 1879 – 1954; Carrington; Cogswell; Devil's Lake – VFW Department Encampment of North Dakota June 10, 11, 12, 1956; Dickinson – Western Hospitality; Fairmount – Peoples State Bank; Fargo – Business Associates, Inc., Goodwill Advertising, American Life Building; AEO, Chicago, 1957, EPKO Photo Supplies; Kiwanis International; Gackle – First State Bank, 50th Anniversary 1903 – 1953; Grand Forks; Grenora; Hope – Methodist Church of Hope, N. Dak. 75th 1880s – 1957; James River – National Bank 75th Anniversary; Kensal; Larimore – 75th Anniversary, Olson Supply; Lisbon – Farmer's State Bank, 1910 – 1960; Minot; North Dakota A. A. G. P. 1959; North Dakota Badlands, Painted Canyon; Portland; Sherwood; Stanley; Sykeston; The Sioux State; Tioga; Wahpeton – Congregational Christian Conference of North Dakota, 75th Anniversary, 1881 – 1956, North Dakota State Barbers Association 1956, North Dakota State Women's Bowling Tournament 1955 – 1956; Williston.

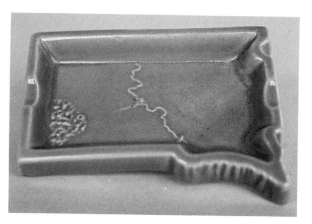

South Dakota map shape, 4½", smaller than original, showing river, $50.00 – 75.00. Also with "THE SUNSHINE STATE."

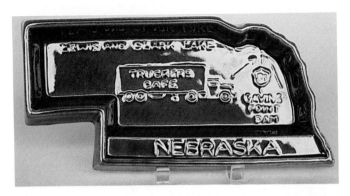

6" Nebraska state map tray, advertising the truckers cafe, $75.00 – 100.00.

4½" Minnesota state map shapes, for an organization and Diamond Jubilee, $50.00 – 75.00 each.

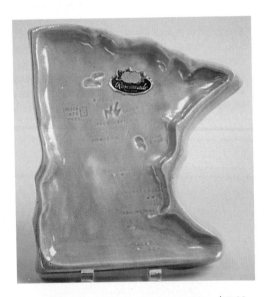

5½" Minnesota plaque in shape of state, $75.00 – 100.00.

Devil's Tower 2" advertising ashtray, $200.00 – 250.00. Devil's Tower National Monument is a natural phenomenon, a great column of rock towering 1,280 feet above the Belle Fourche River in the Wyoming section of the Black Hills.

4¾" Rotary International ashtray, $200.00 – 250.00.

4⅛" Land of Lincoln wall plaque with Lincoln bust, $200.00 – 250.00.

5" advertising ashtrays, $75.00 – 100.00 each. This 5" shape was used for many Rosemeade ashtrays in different colors, although green predominates. Several examples with attached figurines appear in other sections of this book. Others were made for Legion Baseball Capitol, North Dakota, Governor's Proclamation, August 28, 1958, Drayton, N. Dak.; The National Bank, Wahpeton, N. Dak.; and Kenny's Motel and Drive Inn, Jamestown, N. Dak.

Rare wall plaque, Chamber of Commerce Honor Key for Wahpeton, 4⅛" x 7", $300.00+.

5¼" Wahpeton Jaycees ashtray, $150.00 – 200.00.

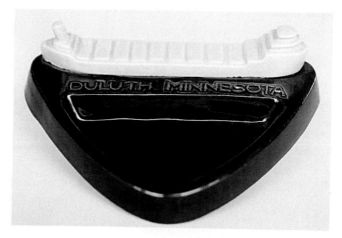

Duluth, Minnesota, ore boat ashtray, $200.00 – 250.00. Also in green without advertising.

Sinclair Lewis' Original Main Street ashtray for Sauk Centre, Minnesota, 5¼", $200.00 – 225.00.

4¾" Ray oil derrick ashtray, for Ray, North Dakota, $150.00 – 200.00. Also for Gambles.

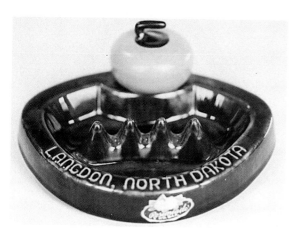

5⅝" ashtray with curling stone, $200.00 – 250.00. According to Joe McLaughlin, sometimes the clay bled through and came out greenish after firing. Other Rosemeade ashtrays also show this tendency. Curling is a Scottish game played on ice in which two four-man teams slide heavy, oblate stones toward a fixed mark in the center of a circle at either end.

Jamestown Bank 75th Anniversary ashtray, 5", $50.00 – 75.00. Also for Legion Baseball Capitol, North Dakota, Governor's Proclamation, August 28, 1958, Drayton, N. Dak.

Wahpeton National Bank ashtray, 7⅛", $75.00 – 100.00.

Money bag-shaped bank ashtrays: 4½" tan and gray Wahpeton bank, $75.00 – 100.00 each; 5½" brown Loretto bank, $100.00 – 125.00.

International Harvester ashtray, 4¼", $200.00 – 250.00.

Walnut Crush ashtray, 8½", $200.00 – 250.00.

Fargo Structural Products triangular ashtray, 6¼", $100.00 – 125.00.

5¼" ashtray for Fergus Lumber and Fuel Co., $100.00 – 125.00.

Mobil logo design on 5" ashtray, a petroliana collectible, $350.00 – 400.00.

5¼" ashtrays for Hoppert's Plumbing and Heating, left, and Waldorf Paper Products, right, $100.00 – 125.00 each.

Phillips 66 logo on 5" ashtray, a petroleum products collectible, $350.00 – 400.00.

4½" advertising ashtray for KOBS Northern Pacific, $100.00 – 150.00.

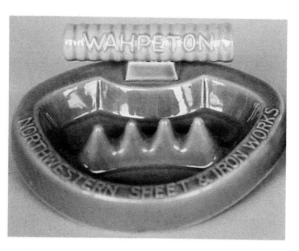

Culvert figurine on 5" advertising ashtray, $175.00 – 200.00.

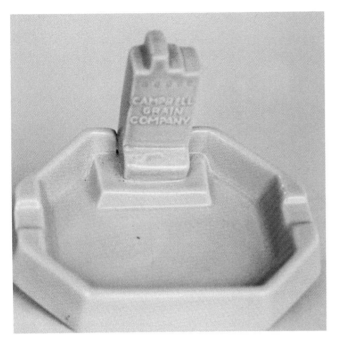

Grain elevator figurine on 4¾" ashtray, $100.00 – 150.00.

Pontiac dealership ashtray, 5½", $150.00 – 200.00. An automobilia collectible.

5" advertising ashtrays: tire figurine, $200.00 – 250.00; bowling ball and pin figurines, $200.00 – 250.00.

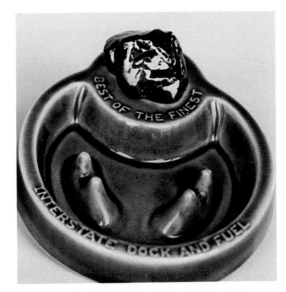

5" advertising ashtray for lignite coal, $200.00 – 250.00. North Dakota has the world's largest deposits of lignite coal, a very soft brown coal.

SPECIAL PIECES

Pottery employees occasionally crafted special items for their friends, relatives or each other. Noticeably different than the standard Rosemeade products, these are commonly known as "lunch hour" pieces. These special pieces meet three criteria. They were made for personal use, in limited quantity, and not as part of a product line. They are important to Rosemeade's story.

Although the Wahpeton Pottery Company and Rosemeade Potteries were commercial ventures, the employees became a family. Tremendous flexibility was allowed at the workplace. One Rosemeade employee mentioned that there was no need to make the special pieces during the lunch hour as employees were free to make them during working hours. Another employee told of taking home pieces to paint.

Special pieces are determined by their provenance (history of origin), or statement by a former employee. They are not priced since they seldom appear on the market. If more examples surface, a piece may need to be reconsidered as part of a product line.

Special pieces made by Rosemeade employees are shown in the following photographs. Some are described with provenance or employee statement.

Joe McLaughlin threw this pitcher and mug set on the wheel as a prototype for Hausauer Beverages. After the Hausauer company decided not to order, this set never went into production. Decals without Les Kouba's name were used.

The provenance of this wildcat mascot indicates that it was made by a Rosemeade employee in 1941 for Wahpeton's State School of Science football team.

This pheasant TV lamp was made by a Rosemeade employee for her sister. After the pheasant was formed in the usual mold, the employee cut the head off and turned it around before firing.

A drawing of this dove is part of Laura Taylor Hughes' papers. The pin was made from sandy clay and unmarked. There is no evidence that the pin ever went into production at Rosemeade.

Sometimes, long after the company's production of a piece, an employee would find the mold and make up another. An example is this pheasant made in the old mold by Joe McLaughlin and painted by the decorators of his era. Color variations may exist with these pieces.

A detailed drawing of this figure exists with Laura Taylor Hughes' papers but it is unknown whether such pieces were part of the Rosemeade product line.

Employees made these white clay, oil-painted versions of the bear stump toothpick holder. The original sandy clay, underglazed, slip-painted piece sold by the company as part of their product lines is on page 125.

Rosemeade shapes that were hand painted in ways different than production line objects are included in this chapter. Some of these may have been painted by Rosemeade employees. However, without documentation or provenance, it is difficult to determine the artist. Bisque ware made at Rosemeade Potteries was widely available in the community (page 42). The following are examples of Rosemeade shapes, hand-painted in ways different than production line objects.

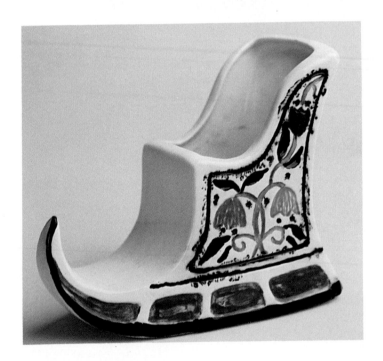

APPENDIX I
Company Booklets

ROSEMEADE OFFERS ITS CUSTOMERS

A WIDE SELECTION

Hand-Thrown Glazed Ware

VASES, *assorted shapes*	$ .50 to 1.00
BUD VASES	.50
CANDLE HOLDERS, *per pair*	1.00
BOWLS	.50 to 2.50
FLOWER BASKETS	.50 to 1.00
PITCHERS	.50 to 1.50
CREAM AND SUGAR SETS	1.00
HATS	.75

Hand-Thrown Bad Lands Ware

VASES AND BOWLS	.50 to 1.50
PITCHERS	.50
CREAM AND SUGAR SETS	1.00
ASH TRAYS	.50 to .75
HATS	.50

Ceramic Figures and Novelty Items

FIGURES, ANIMALS, BIRDS, ETC.	.35 to 10.00
FIGURE AND VASE COMBINATION	1.00 to 2.50
PLAQUES	.75 to 1.25
WALL POCKETS	.50 to 1.50
BOOK-ENDS, *per pair*	3.00 to 4.00
ASH TRAYS	.35 to .75
SALTS AND PEPPERS, *plain and novelty shapes*	.75 to 1.00

> **THE WAHPETON POTTERY CONPANY**
> Was organized in January, 1940 with MR. R. J. HUGHES, a native North Dakotan, as its president. The enthusiastic reception accorded its wares has given the industry a healthy, steady growth. ✳ ✳ ✳ ✳ ✳ ✳ ✳ ✳

Kuelser

Rosemeade
POTTERY

*I saw a potter at his work today
Shaping with rudest hand his whirling clay.
"Ah, gently brother, do not treat me thus;
I, too, was once a man!" I heard it say.*

— OMAR KHAYYAM

ROSEMEADE POTTERY is as native to North Dakota as her state flower— the wild rose—which furnished the inspiration for its name. The fine quality of pottery clay from which it is made comes from near Mandan, North Dakota. Many of the designs were inspired by the state's rose covered meadows, her rolling wheat fields and her scenic Bad Lands. Even the designers of Rosemeade are native North Dakotans . . . . LAURA TAYLOR, manager of the Wahpeton Pottery, creates the original models for the modern ceramic figures as well as the designs for the general line of pottery. VERA GETHMAN of Gorham, North Dakota, uses animals from Wahpeton's Chahinkapa Park as living models for her small naturalistic animal figures; wild horses, which roam at large near her ranch home in the Bad Lands, for her spirited horses . . . . Much of the Rosemeade ware is fashioned on the potter's wheel. This ancient method, known as "throwing", gives each hand-made piece a charm and individuality of its own . . . . Glazes used on the pottery are the result of much experimentation at the Wahpeton factory. Their subdued hues give a suitable finish to the excellent design and fine workmanship which characterize each piece of Rosemeade.

Early Wahpeton Pottery Company Booklet

ROSEMEADE GIFTWARE
A WIDE SELECTION

AMERICAN WILDLIFE NUMBERS—
This group is made up of native birds and animals in the form of salt and pepper sets, wall plaques, ceramic figures and jewelry. The Chinese ring necked pheasant and mallards, with their gay plumage, are particularly lifelike in design and coloring.

FOR FLOWER ARRANGEMENTS—
Rosemeade florists items are decorative as well as useful. There are vases, jardinieres and wall vases in historic Egyptian design with modern styling. Also bowls and candle holders with matching flower holders in bird, fish and animal designs.

CREAM AND SUGAR SETS—
Attractive designs and gay colors characterize these sets. With some of the cream and sugar sets there are matching salts or peppers, ash trays or tea bells.

TEA BELLS—
A tulip bloom with its simple bell shaped form was the inspiration for one of these bells. Others are in the shape of animals or birds. All have musical tones.

BOOKENDS—
The well designed bookends are beautifully glazed in black, brown, wine and bronze. They are weighted and are finished with felt bases. Sturdy and practical, they will really hold books.

The articles mentioned above are only part of the line of beautiful Rosemeade Giftware. There are souvenirs for tourists, items for collectors and gifts for every occasion.

THE WAHPETON POTTERY COMPANY
Wahpeton, North Dakota

Rosemeade
POTTERY

I saw a potter at his work today
Shaping with rudest hand his whirling clay.
"Ah, gently brother, do not treat me thus;
I, too, was once a man!" I heard it say.

—OMAR KHAYYAM

A WORD ABOUT ROSEMEADE GIFTWARE - - -

ROSEMEADE POTTERY is as native to North Dakota as her state flower—The Wild Rose—which furnished the inspiration for its name. A light burning pottery clay of a fine quality from the abundant clay beds of Western North Dakota is used in its manufacture. The pottery designs are the original creations of Laura Taylor Hughes, a native North Dakotan. The state's flower strewn meadows, her scenic Bad Lands, western ranch life and wild game and song birds have inspired many of the pottery designs.

Each piece is first modeled in clay with careful attention given to the outstanding characteristics of the figure which is being made, or to the purpose for which the article is to be used. From the clay models hollow plaster moulds are made. The ware is formed in these moulds by the method known as slip-casting. The clay is prepared by soaking it in water and straining it through a fine sieve. This liquid clay is called slip. The dry mould is filled with slip and it is allowed to stand until a layer of clay has adhered to the inside of the mould. The rest of the slip is poured out and the layer of clay which remains inside becomes the piece of pottery. After the cast piece has been removed from the mould the rough edges are taken off, any imperfections are corrected and the piece is thoroughly dried. It is then given its first or bisque firing. The firing is at a red hot temperature that fuses and hardens the clay and it is then ready for the glazing.

The glaze is a mixture of minerals compounded in such a way that they will melt together when brought to high temperatures. The glaze is applied by dipping, sprayingore brushing and the ware is then returned to th kiln for the second firing, this time at tempetatures even higher than the first. The utmost care is given to each phase of the whole process. Some of the Rosemeade Giftware is finished in softly shaded matt glazes, other pieces in dark bronze or lustrous gloss glazes in colorful hues. The finished product is an article of beauty, of attractive design and fine workmanship; an American product which its manufacturers are proud to offer to admirers of beautiful things.

The Wahpeton Pottery Company, manufacturers of Rosemeade pottery, was organized in 1940 and began business in Wahpeton, North Dakota that year. Its officers are R. J. Hughes, president; Laura Taylor Hughes, treasurer and vice president; and Howard S. Lewis, secretary and production manager.

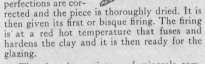

Wahpeton Pottery Company Booklet

APPENDIX II
Sources

The Richland County Historical Museum, Wahpeton, North Dakota, opened July 1, 1965. Its purpose is "to preserve and perpetuate the history of Richland County." A major collection includes Rosemeade pottery, Laura Taylor Hughes' personal pottery collection, photos, and other company memorabilia.

Richland County Historical Museum
Seventh Avenue and Second Street North
Wahpeton, North Dakota 58075
(701) 642-3075

The North Dakota Heritage Center, Bismarck, North Dakota, displays Rosemeade pottery in special exhibits. Located on the state capital grounds since 1981, the center houses the State Museum, State Archives, Historical Research Library and the State Historical Society of North Dakota.

North Dakota Heritage Center
612 East Boulevard
Bismarck, North Dakota 58505
(701) 328-2666

APPENDIX III
North Dakota Pottery
Collectors Society/Commemoratives

The North Dakota Pottery Collectors Society was formed to promote pottery produced in North Dakota, made from North Dakota clay, and completed with North Dakota labor. The purpose of the society is to expand and create an interest in collecting these wares by individuals throughout the United States. The North Dakota potteries include the Wahpeton Pottery Company – Rosemeade Potteries, University of North Dakota

Pottery, Dickinson Clay Products Company, WPA Ceramics, Messer Ceramics, Three Tribes Stoneware, Inc., and Turtle Mountain Pottery. An annual convention, newsletters, and commemorative are membership privileges. Application for NDPCS membership may be made to: North Dakota Pottery Collectors Society; Box 14; Beach, North Dakota 58621

NDPCS logo

1991 paperweight commemorative, 3¼" x 2", decorated with prairie roses and wheat, $200.00+.

2¾" UND-type coyote paperweight commemorative, 1992, $50.00 – 75.00.

4" Dickota-type teepee commemorative, 1993, $150.00 – 200.00.

1994 Rosemeade-type sign, 1¾" x 4" commemorative, $150.00 – 200.00.

3" mallard drake commemorative pin, 1997, $150.00 – 200.00.

1995 Rosemeade-type bison commemorative, 3½" x 3½", $50.00 – 75.00

4¼" plate commemorative with capitol motif, 1996, $75.00 – 100.00.

1998 Dickota dealer sign commemorative, 3¼" x 3", $75.00 – 100.00.

1999 commemorative salt/pepper shakers for Rosemeade open house, 2⅜", $25.00 – 50.00.

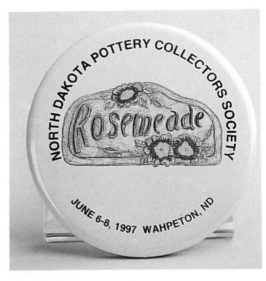

1997 convention button pin with Rosemeade tradename, 2¼", $5.00 – 10.00.

1999 convention button pin with Rosemeade design, 2¼", $5.00 – 10.00.

6½" tray with Rosemeade mice figurines used as 1999 convention door prize, $50.00 – 75.00.

APPENDIX IV
Questionable Items

The following guidelines have been used to identify verifiable Rosemeade pottery: company promotional materials like stock lists and advertisements; company sales literature, like invoices and sales letters; authentication by two or more former employees in positions to know or indelible company marks. Questionable items do not meet these guidelines. These questionable items also do not meet the special pieces criteria. Many pieces, thought to be Rosemeade pottery, have been made by Dryden Pottery, Rushmore Pottery or Frankoma Pottery as the clay color is similar, and they were made in the same time period.

Also, as discussed in the collecting chapter, a major problem is the number of Rosemeade stickers which seem to have been freely distributed.

Some collectors have perceived the following items to be Rosemeade products, but they remain questionable. Hopefully, further research will provide the answers.

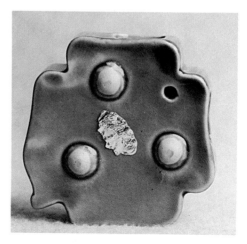

At this time, little documentation has been found to show that the 4-H wall pocket was made as part of the Rosemeade pottery line. Some research seems to indicate that it was made by Dryden Pottery of Ellsworth, Kansas. Several examples have surfaced, but none with a company ink stamp mark. RIGHT: Bottom of 4-H wall pocket.

4" Boy Scout mug

These salt/pepper shakers are larger than the Flex-Mold figurine on page 130, made by the company. They look similar, but no documentation has been found regarding their production as Rosemeade pottery. Only one pair has surfaced.

Although a Mount Rushmore figurine was made as part of Rosemeade's product line (page 135), these bookends are different. Since there is a lack of documentation that they were produced at Rosemeade Potteries, additional research is needed.

As the Golden Gloves boxing competition was held at the State College of Science for 48 years, many contestants, family members, and fans converged in Wahpeton every year. Rosemeade Potteries, perceiving a marketing opportunity, may have produced boxing glove souvenirs for visitors to the city.

ENDNOTES

HISTORY

1. P. D. Norton, *State of North Dakota: 1911 Legislative Manual* (Bismarck, North Dakota: Tribune, State Printers and Binders, 1912), 147.

2. Ella Grandlund Mathiesen, *Rosemeade North Dakota: Precious Memories* (self-published, 1981), 3.

3. Laura Taylor Hughes, papers, speeches and correspondence at the Richland County Historical Society.

4. Erling Nicolai Rolfsrud, "Rosemeade Lady," *Our Young People*, Volume 33, Number 12, (March 20, 1955).

5. Hughes, papers.

6. Ibid.

7. Ibid.

8. Ibid.

9. Ibid.

10. Erling N. Rolfsrud, "The Top Drawer," *North Dakota Teacher.*

11. Margaret Cable, personal papers on file at the Elwyn B. Robinson Department of Special Collections, Chester Fritz Library, University of North Dakota, Grand Forks, North Dakota.

12. "Lion of N.D. Clay Pleases Club Head," *The Bismarck Tribune* (December 14, 1933), 3.

13. "Ceramics Development Project Funds Ready Response Here," *Dickinson Press* (September 10, 1936).

14. Ibid.

15. Ibid.

16. "De Lamere Lady Heads Ceramic Department Project at Dickinson," *Dickinson Press* (August 1936).

17. Karen McCready, *Art Deco and Modernist Ceramics* (New York: Thames and Hudson, Inc., 1995), 29.

18. "All the World's a Fair: The Modern Age," exhibition, the Wolfsonian Foundation, Miami Beach, Florida, January, 1999.

19. Erling Nicolai Rolfsrud, *Extraordinary North Dakotans* (Alexandria, Minnesota: Lantern Books, 1954), 202.

20. Hughes, papers.

21. "Laura Taylor Hughes, Written by Herself," paper at Richland County Historical Museum, 1.

22. Hughes, papers.

23. Ibid.

24. Ibid.

25. "North Dakota Produces the Materials for a New Capitol," brochure, Greater North Dakota Association, Fargo, North Dakota, 1931.

26. Marion J. Piper, *Dakota Portraits* (Mohall, North Dakota, 1964), 121.

27. Hughes, papers.

28. Ibid.

29. "Wahpeton Pottery Company Open House Friday," *Richland County Farmer-Globe* (October 18, 1940), front page.

30. "Seven Hundred Women Attend Pottery Open House," *Richland County Farmer-Globe* (October 22, 1940), front page.

31. Hughes, papers.

32. "Laura Taylor Hughes," 3.

33. Hughes, papers.

34. "Laura Taylor Hughes," 3.

35. Rolfsrud, *Extraordinary North Dakotans,* 202.

36. Bobbie Forester, "Workers in Clay." *Arkansas Gazette* (September 11, 1932), 5.

37. Vernon E. Hektner, Dean Emeritus, NDSCS, speech presented to North Dakota Pottery Collectors Society, June 11, 1994, 6.

38. Warren Olson, interview.

39. Phil Penas, "North Dakota Clay Used in Wahpeton Pottery Business," *Fargo Forum* (May 31, 1953), 22.

40. Scrapbook of Olga Hektner, on file at the Richland County Historical Museum.

41. Hughes, papers.

42. Hughes, papers.

43. Penas, 22.

44. Maureen Donnelly, "Palm Trees and Banana Leaves: Pottery Decoration in Subtropical New Orleans," *Style 1900*, Volume 12, Number 1 (Winter/Spring 1999), 44.

45. Hughes, papers.

46. Marion John Nelson, *Art Pottery of the Midwest* (Minneapolis: University Art Museum, University of Minnesota, 1988), 75 & 76.

47. Martin Eidelberg, "Myths of Style and Nationalism: American Art Pottery at the Turn of the Century," *The Journal of Decorative and Propaganda Arts* (Volume 20, 1994), 111.

48. Jessie Poesch, *Newcomb Pottery: An Enterprise for Southern Women, 1885–1940.* (Exton, Pennsylvania: Schiffer Publishing, Ltd., 1984), 66.

49. Eidelberg, 97.

50. Hughes, papers.

51. Madeline Marsh, *Collecting the 1950s* (London: Reed Books Limited, 1997), 54.

52. David P. Gray and Gerald G. Newborg, *North Dakota: a pictorial history* (Norfolk, Virginia: The Donning Company, 1988), 233.

53. North Dakota tourism brochure.

54. John James Audubon and Rev. John Bachman, *The Imperial Collection of Audubon Animals* (New York: Bonanza Books, 1967), 69.

55. Hughes, papers.

56. Hughes, papers.

57. "Bambi Proves Popular with Public: Pottery Figurines Carry Greeting," *Richland County Farmer-Globe* (December 23, 1952), front page.

58. "At Your Service," *The Gift and Art Buyer* (June 1949), 142.

59. "At Your Service," *The Gift and Art Buyer* (August 1950), 210.

60. Hughes, papers.

61. Hughes, papers.

ENDNOTES

62. Leo A. Borah and J. Baylor Roberts, "North Dakota Comes into Its Own," *The National Geographic Magazine* (September 1951), 306.

63. Hughes, papers.

64. Hughes, papers.

65. Penas, 22.

66. Melinda Burris Willms, "A Practical Spirituality: Merchandising Mountain Handicraft," *Style 1900* (Winter/Spring 1999), 63.

67. *Decorative Arts: Official Catalog,* Department of Fine Arts, Division of Decorative Arts; Golden Gate International Exposition (San Francisco: San Francisco Bay Exposition Company, 1939), 32.

68. Hughes, papers.

69. Hughes, papers.

70. "Rosemeade Potteries Is New Name for Local Pottery," *Richland County Farmer-Globe* (February 10, 1952), 2.

71. Howard Lewis, speech to North Dakota Pottery Collectors Society, June 9, 1991.

72. Joe McLaughlin, interview.

73. McLaughlin, interview.

74. Penas, 22.

75. Susan M. Larson, "Interested in Rosemeade Pottery? Howard Lewis Helped the Wahpeton Pottery Company Grow," *Wahpeton Daily News* (January 1991).

76. McLaughlin, interview.

77. Betty McLaughlin, interview.

78. "Laura Taylor Hughes," 4.

79. Hektner, 3.

PROCESS/SWIRL

1. "Laura Taylor Hughes," 2.

2. Margaret Cable, "Possibilities of Pottery Making from North Dakota Clays," paper for North Dakota Federation of Womens' Clubs Art in North Dakota Series, undated, 17.

3. Hughes, papers.

4. "Rosemeade Pottery" booklet.

5. "Mandan Clay made into Rosemeade Art Pottery at Wahpeton," *North Dakotan* (December 1940), 4.

6. Hughes, papers.

7. Hughes, papers

8. Cable, "Possibilities of Pottery Making," 17.

9. Cable, papers.

10. David Harris Cohen and Catherine Hess, *Looking at European Ceramics: A Guide to Technical Terms* (Malibu, California: The J. Paul Getty Museum, 1993), 61.

11. Hughes, papers.

12. Michael Casson, *The Craft of the Potter* (London: British Broadcasting Corporation, 1977), 97.

13. Provoslov Rada, *Book of Ceramics* (London: Spring Books, 1962), 97.

14. "Laura Taylor Hughes," 2.

15. Penas, 22.

16. "Laura Taylor Hughes," 2.

17. Emma Althoff, interview.

18. Laurie J. Kassell, "Rosemeade pottery exhibit," *Daily News* (September 7, 1990).

19. Cable, papers.

20. Regina Lee Blaszczyt, "The Aesthetic Movement: China Decorators, Consumer Demand and Technological Change in the American Pottery Industry, 1865 – 1900," *Winterthur Portfolio*, Volume 29, Numbers 2/3 (Summer Autumn, 1994), 150.

21. Grant Beach, "Pointers for Potters," *Popular Ceramics* (May 1965), 78.

22. Hugo Morley-Fletcher, Consultant Editor, *Techniques of the World's Great Masters of Pottery and Porcelain* (London: Chartwell Books. 1984), 30.

23. McLaughlin, interview.

24. Norman Karlson, *American Art Tile* (New York: Rizzoli International Publications, Inc., 1998), 109.

25. McLaughlin, interview.

26. Emma Althoff, interview.

27. Morley-Fletcher, 30.

28. Cable, "Possibilities of Pottery Making," 18.

29. "Laura Taylor Hughes," 2.

30. Hughes, papers.

31. "Mandan Clay," 4.

32. "Mandan Clay," 4.

33. Lewis, interview.

34. Nelson, 75.

35. Hughes, papers.

36. Cable, "Possibilities of Pottery Making," 18.

37. Ibid.

38. Hughes, papers.

39. Hughes, papers.

40. Lois Lehner, *Encyclopedia of U.S. Marks on Pottery, Porcelain and Clay* (Paducah, Kentucky: Collector Books, 1988) 319.

COLLECTING

1. Shirley Sampson and Irene Harms, *Beautiful Rosemeade* (Garretson, South Dakota: Sanders Printing Company, 1987) 7.

2. Hughes, papers.

3. "Wahpeton Only Place In Nation Selling Rosemeade Seconds," *Richland County Farmer-Globe* (May 1, 1953).

4. "Birdies Sing in New Designs," *Richland County Farmer-Globe* (November 13, 1951).

5. Delores Berg, interview.

6. James Mackay, *Collectables* (London: Macdonald and Jane's, 1979), 22.

7. Wendy Bounds, "Don't Throw Out That Old Ashtray Yet," *The Wall Street Journal* (June 26, 1997), 1.

8. Philip Collins, *Smokerama: Classic Tobacco Accoutrements* (San Francisco: Chronicle Books, 1992), 3.

9. Ibid.

10. Richard G. Racheter, "Ladies and Gentlemen: Light Up!" *The Daze Inc.* (March 1997), 7.

11. Peter J. Theriault, "The Jewels Stop Here," *Maine Antique Digest* (November 1998), 28F.

12. Ruth H. Randall, *Ceramic Sculpture* (New York Watson-Guptill Publications, Inc., 1951), 78.

13. Don Duer, *A Penny Saved: Still and Mechanical Banks* (Atglen, Pennsylvania: Schiffer Publishing Ltd.,1993), Forward.

14. Savi Arbola and Marco Onesti, *Piggy Banks,* (San Francisco: Chronicle Books, 1992), 3.

15. William C. Ketchum, Jr., *Western Memorabilia Collectibles of the Old West* (Maplewood, New Jersey: Rutledge Books Inc., 1982), Introduction.

16. Harry L. Rinker, "50s culture required a figural lamp atop every TV set," *Antique Week* (March 30, 1998), 9.

17. Marsh, 39.

18. Ted Hake, *Hake's Guide to TV Collectibles* (Radnor, Pennsylvania: Wallace-Homestead Book Company, 1990) vi.

19. Fredda Perkins, "Wall Pockets: Wall Hung Vases From The Past," *The Antique Traveler Newspaper* (September 1995), 21.

20. Robert Reed, "Wall pockets," *Collector News* (March 1996), 13.

21. Perkins, 26.

22. Robert Seecof and Donna Lee Seecof, "Bookends Belong To America," *Antiques and Collecting* (March 1998), 37.

23. Robert Reed, "Bookends: Two of a Kind Collectibles," *Collectors News* (June 1997), 6.

24. Tina Rickey, "These pots are flowering in collectors' homes," *Antique Week* (September 14, 1998), 1.

25. John L. Gilbert, "19th Century Candlesticks and Candle Lamps," *The Antique Traveler* (Dubuque, Iowa: The Antique Trader, 1977), 4.

26. Norma L. Walker, "The Lure of the Lamp," *Antiques and Collecting* (March 1999), 27.

27. Margaret Ballard, "Animal Bells," *The Antiques Journal* (April 1974), 32.

28. Darlene Dommel, "Fermenting: Breweriana," *The Antiques Journal* (April 1974), 58.

29. Ann Barry Burrows, "Two of A Kind," *Collector* (September 1994), 20.

30. Mike Schneider, *The Complete Salt and Pepper Shakers Book* (Atglen, Pennsylvania: Schiffer Publishing, Ltd., 1993), 9.

31. Schneider, 154.

32. Rosemeade Pottery Company booklet.

33. "Governor Lauds Local Artist at Bismarck Meeting," *Bismarck Tribune* (November 1951).

PRODUCT LINES

Pheasants
1. Hughes, papers.
2. Hughes, papers.
3. "Souvenir Birds Prove Popular with Hunters," *Richland County Farmer-Globe,* November 6, 1945, 1.
4. Wahpeton Pottery Company advertisement.
5. Hughes, papers.
6. Ibid.
7. Ibid.
8. Mackay, 42

Ducks/Geese
1. Darlene Pfister, "In the prairie, potholes are good," *Star Tribune* (August 8, 1998), B1.
2. Joan Marie Verba, *North Dakota* (Minneapolis, Minnesota: Lerner Publications Company, 1992), 55.
3. Gray, 230.

Chickens
1. Howard F. Robinson, Editor, *The Gift of Birds* (Washington, D.C.: National Wildlife Federation, 1979), 69.
2. Robinson, 69.

Turkeys
1. Company advertisement.

Other Birds
1. John P. Cushiom, *Animals in Pottery and Porcelain* (New York: Crown Publishers, Inc., 1974), 9.
2. Hughes, papers.

Fish/Marine
1. Art Hutt, "It Looks Good To Me," *Fisherman* (December 1952), 6.
2. Hughes, papers.
3. Ibid.

Les Kouba
1. Les Kouba interview.
2. "A Wild Heart, A Very Disciplined Art," *Southwestern Journal* (November 26, 1986), 35.
3. Kouba interview.

Floral/Foliage
1. Morley-Fletcher, 129.

2. Robert L. Polley, Editor, *America The Beautiful In The Words of Henry David Thoreau* (New York: William Morrow and Company, 1966), 91.
3. Jocasta Innes, *The Country Pottery Companion* (San Francisco: Collins Publishers, 1995), 53.
4. Hughes, papers.

Agricultural
1. *Mobile Travel Guide: Northwest and Great Plains* (New York: Foder's Travel Publications, Inc., 1977), 119.
2. Fred A. Newton, *Bass and Bugs, Crabs and Crawlers, and the Folks Who Chase Them* (Two Rivers, Wisconsin: Siskiwit Press, 1997), 126.

Dogs
1. Bill Tarrant, *The Magic of Dogs* (New York: Lyons-Burford, 1995), 3.
2. David Taylor, *The Ultimate Dog Book* (New York: Simon and Schuster, 1990), 10.
3. Taylor, 6.
4. Hughes, papers.

Cats
1. J.L. Lynnlee, *Purr-fection: The Cat* (West Chester, Pennsylvania: Schiffer Publishing Ltd., 1990), 5.

Horses
1. Appleton Museum of Art, "The Horse in Fine Art," *Antiques and Art Around Florida* (Summer/Fall 1997), 10.
2. Laura Taylor Hughes, "The Potter's Art," *North Dakota Horticulture* (January 1947), 11.

Farm Animals
1. Melva Davern, *The Collector's Encyclopedia of Salt and Pepper Shakers: Figural and Novelty* (Paducah, Kentucky: Collector Books, 1991), 28.
2. *Mobile Guide,* 179.

Deer
1. "Bambi Proves Popular," front page.
2. Ibid.

Bison
1. Michael S. Sample, *Bison: Symbol of the American West* (Helena, Montana: Falcon Press, 1987), 31.
2. Sample, 26.

ENDNOTES

Other Wildlife

1. Warner Shedd, *The Kid's Wildlife Book* (Charlotte, Vermont: Williamson Publishing, 1994), 6.

2. Audubon, 269.

3. Conrad W. Leifur, *Our State North Dakota* (New York: American Book Company, 1953), 73.

4. Audubon, 69.

5. Merle Severy, Editor, *Wild Animals of North America* (Chicago: National Geographic Society, 1960), 247.

6. Hughes, papers.

7. Durward L. Allen, *The Life of Prairies and Plains* (New York: McGraw-Hill Book Company, 1967), 91.

8. Tom Dickson, "Oh Deer!" *The Minnesota Volunteer* (September – October 1996), 26.

9. Hughes, papers.

Theodore Roosevelt

1. Federal Workers Project, *North Dakota: A Guide to the Northern Prairie State* (Oxford, England: Oxford University Press, 1950), 175.

2. Henry A. Schoch and Bruce M. Kaye, *Theodore Roosevelt National Park: The Story Behind the Scenery* (Las Vegas, Nevada: KC Publications, 1993), 5.

3. Schoch, 47.

4. Zena Irma Trinka, *North Dakota of Today* (St. Paul, Minnesota: Louis F. Dow Co., 1920), Preface.

5. Robin McMacken, *The Dakotas: Off The Beaten Track* (Old Saybrook, Connecticut: The Globe Pequot Press, 1996), x.

6. Josa Keyes, *The Teddy Bear Story* (New York: Gallery Books, 1985), 8.

7. "The Medorian," newspaper published by the Theodore Roosevelt Medora Foundation, Medora, North Dakota, Summer edition, 1998.

Place Souvenirs

1. William Morris, *The American Heritage Dictionary of the English Language* (Boston: Houghton Mifflin Company, 1976), 904.

2. Robert Famighetti, *The World Almanac* (Mahwah, New Jersey: Funk and Wagnalls Corporation, 1996), 543.

3. Bertha Rachel Palmer, *Beauty Spots in North Dakota* (Boston: The Gorham Press, 1928), 141.

4. J. Signe Snortland, *A Traveler's Companion to North Dakota State Historic Sites* (Bismarck, North Dakota: State Historical Society of North Dakota, 1996), 114.

Egyptian

1. Company advertisement.

2. Company advertisement.

3. Company advertisement.

4. Company advertisement.

Human Forms

1. Hughes, papers.

2. Ibid.

3. "Sunny Nodak Grows 'N' Grows," *North Dakotan* (October 1957), 2.

4. Ibid.

Native Americans

1. Snortland, 44.

2. Taylor, papers.

Accessories

1. William C. Ketchum Jr., *Western Memorabilia: Collectibles of the Old West* (Maplewood, New Jersey: Rutledge Books, Inc., 1980), 105.

Functional

1. Charles F. Binns, "Clay in the Potter's Hand," *The Craftsman*, paper on file at the Elwyn B. Robinson Department of Special Collections, Chester Fritz Library, University of North Dakota, Grand Forks, North Dakota, 164.

2. "And once there were no handles," *The Antique Journal* (October 1998), 25.

3. Michael J. Goldberg, "Getting in Solid," *American Country Collectibles* (March 1998), 34.

BIBLIOGRAPHY

"A Wild Heart, A Very Disciplined Art," *Southwest Journal*, November 26, December 9, 1986, page 35.

Allen, Durward L. *The Life of Prairies and Plains.* New York: McGraw-Hill Book Company, 1967.

"All The World's A Fair: The Modern Age," exhibition, The Wolf-sonian Foundation, Miami Beach, Florida, January, 1999.

"And once there were no handles," *The Antique Journal*, October, 1998, page 25.

Appleton Museum of Art, "The Horse in Fine Art," *Antiques and Art Around Florida*, Summer/Fall, 1997, page 10.

Arbola, Savi and Marco Onesti. *Piggy Banks.* San Francisco: Chronicle Books, 1992.

"At Your Service," *The Gift and Art Buyer*, June, 1949, page 142.

"At Your Service," *The Gift and Art Buyer*, August, 1950, page 210.

Audubon, John James and Rev. John Bachman. *The Imperial Collection of Audubon Animals.* New York: Bonanza Books, 1967.

Ballard, Margaret. "Animal Bells," *The Antiques Journal*, April 1974, pages 32 – 34.

Bank, Mort. *The North Dakota Fishing Guide.* Bismarck, North Dakota: Bismark Tribune, 1977.

"Bambi Proves Popular with Public: Pottery Figurines Carry Greeting," *Richland County Farmer-Globe*, December 23, 1952, front page.

Barr, Paul E. *North Dakota Artists.* Grand Forks, North Dakota: University of North Dakota Library, 1954.

Barr, Sir John Lubbock. *The Pleasures of Life.* Chicago: M. A. Donohue and Company, 1887.

Bassett, Mark and Victoria Naumann. *Cowan Pottery and the Cleveland School.* Atglen, Pennsylvania: Schiffer Publishing Ltd., 1997.

Beach, Grant. "Pointers for Potters," *Popular Ceramics*, May, 1965, page 78.

Berg, Francie M. *North Dakota: Land of Changing Seasons.* Hettinger, North Dakota, Flying Diamond Books, 1989.

Berges, Ruth. *The Collector's Cabinet.* New York: A. S. Barnes and Company, Inc., 1980.

Biek, Robert F. *A Visitor's Guide to the North Dakota Capitol Grounds.* Bismarck, North Dakota: State Historical Society of North Dakota, 1995.

Binns, Charles F. "Clay in the Potter's Hand," *The Craftsman*, paper on file at The Elwyn B. Robinson Department of Special Collections, Chester Fritz Library, University of North Dakota, Grand Forks, North Dakota, pages 162 – 168.

Binns, Charles F. *The Potter's Craft.* Princeton, New Jersey: D. Van Norstrand Company, Inc., 1910.

"Birdies Sing in New Design," *Richland County Farmer-Globe*, November 13, 1951.

Birks, Tony. *The Complete Potter's Companion.* New York: Little, Brown and Company, 1998.

Blaszczyk, Regina Lee. "The Aesthetic Moment: China Decorators, Consumer Demand and Technological Change in the American Pottery Industry, 1865 – 1900," *Winterthur Portfolio*, Summer/Autumn, 1994, Volume 29, Numbers 2/3, pages 121 – 153.

Borah, Leo A. and J. Baylor Roberts. "North Dakota Comes into Its Own," *The National Geographic Magazine*, September, 1951.

Bounds, Wendy. "Don't Throw Out That Old Ashtray Yet," *The Wall Street Journal*, June 26, 1997, pages 1, 10.

Burrows, Ann Barry. "Two Of A Kind," *Collector*, September, 1994, page 20.

Cable, Margaret. personal papers on file at the Elwyn B. Robinson Department of Special Collections, Chester Fritz Library, University of North Dakota, Grand Forks, North Dakota.

Cable, Margaret. "Possibilities of Pottery Making from North Dakota Clays," paper for North Dakota Federation of Womens' Clubs Art in North Dakota Series, undated.

Casson, Michael. *The Craft of the Potter.* London: British Broadcasting Corporation, 1977.

"Ceramics Development Project Finds Ready Response Here," Dickinson Press, September 10, 1936.

Cohen, David Harris and Catherine Hess. *Looking at European Ceramics: A Guide to Technical Terms.* Malibu, California: The J. Paul Getty Museum, 1993.

Collins, Philip. *Smokerama: Classic Tobacco Accoutrements.* San Francisco: Chronicle Books, 1992.

Cushion, John P. *Animals in Pottery and Porcelain.* New York: Crown Publishers, Inc., 1974.

Davern, Melva. *The Collector's Encyclopedia of Salt and Pepper Shakers: Figural and Novelty.* Paducah, Kentucky: Collector Books, 1991.

BIBLIOGRAPHY

"De Lamere Lady Heads Ceramic Department Project at Dickinson," *Dickinson Press*, August, 1936.

Decorative Arts: Official Catalog Department of Fine Arts Division of Decorative Arts, Golden Gate International Exposition. San Francisco: San Francisco Bay Exposition Company, 1939.

Dickson, Tom. "Oh Deer!" *The Minnesota Volunteer*, September – October 1996, pages 19 – 27.

Dommel, Darlene Hurst. *Collector's Encyclopedia of Howard Pierce Porcelain*. Paducah, Kentucky: Collector Books, 1998.

Dommel, Darlene Hurst. *Collector's Encyclopedia of the Dakota Potteries*. Paducah, Kentucky: Collector Books, 1996.

Dommel, Darlene. "Fermenting: Breweriana," *The Antiques Journal*, April, 1974, pages 28 – 30, 58.

Donnelly, Maureen. "Palm Trees and Banana Leaves: Pottery Decoration in Subtropical New Orleans," *Style 1900*, Winter/Spring, 1999, Volume 12, Number 1, pages 42 – 48.

Duer, Don. *A Penny Saved: Still and Mechanical Banks*. Atglen, Pennsylvania: Schiffer Publishing Ltd., 1993.

Eidelberg, Martin. "Myths of Style and Nationalism: American Art Pottery at the Turn of the Century," *The Journal of Decorative and Propaganda Arts*, Volume 20, 1994.

Famighetti, Robert, Editor. *The World Almanac and Book of Facts 1996*. Mahwah, New Jersey: Funk and Wagnalls Corporation, 1996.

Federal Workers Project. *North Dakota: A Guide to the Northern Prairie State*, Oxford, England: Oxford University Press, 1950.

Fish, Herbert Clay. *A Brief History of North Dakota*. New York: American Book Company, 1926.

Forester, Bobbie. "Workers in Clay," *Arkansas Gazette*, September 11, 1932, page 5.

Gilbert, John L. "19th Century Candlesticks and Candle Lamps," *The Antique Trader Annual of Articles Volume V*. Dubuque, Iowa, 1977, pages 4, 5.

Goldberg, Michael J. "Getting in Solid," *American Country Collectibles*, March, 1998, pages 32 – 35, 74 – 76.

"Governor Lauds Local Artist at Bismarck Meeting," *Bismarck Tribune*, November 1951.

Grassick, J. Along the Way brochure, Grand Forks, North Dakota 1932.

Gray, David P. and Gerald G. North Newborg. *Dakota: a pictorial history*. Norfolk, Virginia: The Donning Company, 1988.

Gray, Dick. *Passwords for all Seasons*. Minneapolis, Minnesota: Freshwater Biological Research Foundation, 1973.

Hake, Ted. *Hake's Guide to TV Collectibles*. Radnor, Pennsylvania, Wallace-Homestead Book Company, 1990.

Hektner, Vernon E. Speech presented to North Dakota Pottery Association, June 11, 1994.

Hiesinger, Kathryn B. and George H. Marcus. *Antique Speak: A Guide to the Styles, Techniques, and Materials of the Decorative Arts*. New York: Abbeville Press, 1997.

Honey, W. B. *The Art of the Potter*. London: Faber and Faber, 1946.

Horn, Richard. *Fifties styles: then and now*. New York: Beech Tree Books, 1985.

Hughes, Laura Taylor. Papers, speeches, and correspondence at the Richland County Historical Museum.

Hughes, Laura Taylor. "The Potter's Art," *North Dakota Horticulture*, January 1947, page 11.

Hutt, Art. "It Looks Good To Me," *Fisherman*, December, 1952.

Innes, Jocasta. *The Country Pottery Companion*. San Francisco: Collins Publishers, 1995.

Kardon, Janet, Editor. *Craft In the Machine Age*. New York: Harry N. Abrams, 1995.

Karlson, Norman. *American Art Tile*. New York: Rizzoli, International Publications, Inc., 1998.

Kassell, Laurie L. "Rosemeade pottery exhibit," *Daily News*, September 7, 1990.

Kazeck, Melvin E. *North Dakota: A Human and Economic Geography*. Fargo, North Dakota: North Dakota Agricultural College, 1956.

Ketchum, William C., Jr. *Western Memorabilia: Collectibles of the Old West*. Maplewood, New Jersey: Rutledge Books, Inc., 1980.

Keyes, Josa. *The Teddy Bear Story*. New York: Gallery Books, 1985.

Knue, Joseph. *North Dakota Wildlife Viewing Guide*. Helena, Montana: Falcon Press Publishing Co., Inc., 1992.

Larson, Susan M. "Interested in Rosemeade Pottery? Howard Lewis Helped the Wahpeton Pottery Company Grow," *Wahpeton Daily News*, January, 1991.

"Laura Taylor Hughes, Written by Herself," paper at Richland County Historical Museum.

Lehner, Lois. *Lehner's Encyclopedia of the U. S. Marks on Pottery, Porcelain and Clay*. Paducah, Kentucky: Collector Books, 1988.

Leifur, Conrad W. *Our State North Dakota*. New York: American Book Company, 1953.

Lewis, Howard. Speech to North Dakota Pottery Collectors Society at annual convention, June 9, 1991.

"Lion of N. D. Clay Pleases Club Head," *The Bismarck Tribune,* December 14, 1933, page 3.

Lynnlee, J. L. *Purrfection: The Cat.* Westchester, Pennsylvania: Schiffer Publishing Ltd., 1990.

Mackay, James. *An Encyclopedia of Small Antiques.* New York: Harper and Row, Publishers, 1975.

Mackay, James. *Collectables.* London: MacDonald and Jane's, 1979.

"Mandan Clay Made into Rosemeade Art Pottery at Wahpeton," *North Dakotan,* December 1940, page 4.

Manroe, Candace Ord. *Designing with Collectibles.* New York: Simon and Schuster, 1992.

Marsh, Madeline. *Collecting the 1950s.* London: Reed Books Limited, 1997.

Mathieson, Ella Grandlund. *Rosemeade North Dakota: Precious Memories.* Self-Published, 1981.

McCready, Karen. *Art Deco and Modernist Ceramics.* New York: Thames and Hudson Inc., 1995.

McMacken, Robin. *The Dakotas – Off The Beaten Track.* Old Saybrook, Connecticut: The Globe Pequot Press, 1996.

Mobil Travel Guide: Northwest and Great Plains. New York: Fodor's Travel Publications, Inc., 1997.

Morley-Fletcher, Hugo, Consultant Editor. *Techniques of the World's Great Masters of Pottery and Porcelain.* London: Chartwell Books, 1984.

Morris, William, Editor. *The American Heritage Dictionary of the English Language.* Boston: Houghton Mifflin Company, 1976.

Nelson, Glenn C. *Ceramics.* New York: Holt, Rinehart and Winston, 1960.

Nelson, Marion John. *Art Pottery of the Midwest.* Minneapolis: University Art Museum, University of Minnesota, 1988.

Newton, Fred A. *Bass and Bugs, Crabs and Crawlers, and The Folks Who Chase Them.* Two Rivers, Wisconsin: Siskiwit Press, 1997.

"North Dakota Produces the Materials for a New Capitol," brochure, Greater North Dakota Association, Fargo, North Dakota, 1931.

North Dakota tourism brochure.

Norton, P. D. *State of North Dakota: 1911 Legislative Manual.* Bismarck, North Dakota: Tribune, State Printers and Binders, 1912.

Palmer, Bertha Rachel. *Beauty Spots in North Dakota.* Boston: The Gorham Press, 1928.

Penas, Phil. "North Dakota Clay Used in Wahpeton Pottery Business," *Fargo Forum,* May 31, 1953, page 22.

Perkins, Fredda, "Wall Pockets: Wall Hung Vases From The Past," *The Antique Traveler Newspaper,* September, 1995, pages 21, 26, 30.

Pfister, Darlene. "In the prairie, potholes are good," *Star Tribune,* August 8, 1998, page B1.

Piper, Marion J. *Dakota Portraits.* Mohall, North Dakota: self-published, 1964.

Poesch, Jessie. *Newcomb Pottery: An Enterprise for Southern Women, 1985 – 1940.* Exton, Pennsylvania: Schiffer Publishing, Ltd., 1984.

Polley, Robert L., Editor. *America the Beautiful In the Words of Henry David Thoreau.* New York: William Morrow and Company, 1966.

Racheter, Richard G. "Ladies and Gentlemen: Light Up!" *The Daze Inc.,* March, 1997, page 7.

Rada, Pravoslav. *Book of Ceramics.* London: Spring Books, 1962.

Randall, Ruth H. *Ceramic Sculpture.* New York: Watson-Guptill Publications, Inc., 1951.

Rawson, Phillip, "The Values of Craft," lecture sponsored by the Northern Clay Center and held at Walker Art Center, September, 1993.

Reed, Robert, "Bookends: Two of a Kind Collectibles," *Collectors News,* June 1997, pages 6, 7.

Reed, Robert. "Wall Pockets" *Collector News,* March 1996, pages 12, 13.

Richey, Tina. "These pots are flowering in collectors' homes," *Antique Week,* September 14, 1998, pages 1, 48.

Rinker, Harry L. "50s culture required a figural lamp atop every TV set," *Antique Week,* March 30, 1998, page 9.

Robinson, Elwyn B. *History of North Dakota.* Lincoln, Nebraska: University of Nebraska Press, 1966.

Robinson, Howard F., Editor. *The Gift of Birds.* Washington, D.C.: National Wildlife Federation, 1979.

Rolfstrud, Erling N. "The Top Drawer," *North Dakota Teacher.*

Rolfstrud, Erling Nicolai. "Rosemeade Lady," *Our Young People,* Number 12, Volume 33, March 20, 1955.

"Rosemeade – Famous Name In Pottery," *Hi Lites,* October, 1995, Volume IV, Number 10, page 6.

"Rosemeade Potteries is New Name for Local Pottery," *Richland County Farmer-Globe,* February 10, 1953, page 2.

Rosemeade Pottery company booklet.

Royal Doulton Potteries. *Royal Doulton Figurines.* Stoke-on-Trent, England: Royal Doulton Potteries, 1967.

BIBLIOGRAPHY

Sample, Michael S. *Bison: Symbol of the American West.* Helena, Montana: Falcon Press, 1987.

Sampson, Shirley and Irene J. Harms. *Beautiful Rosemeade.* Garretson, South Dakota: Sanders Printing Company, 1987.

Schneider, Mike. *The Complete Salt and Pepper Shaker Book.* Atglen, Pennsylvania: Schiffer Publishing, Ltd., 1993.

Schoch, Henry A. and Bruce M. Kaye. *Theodore Roosevelt National Park: The Story Behind the Scenery.* Las Vegas, Nevada: K C Publications, 1993.

Scrapbook of Olga Hektner, former Rosemeade employee, on file at the Richland County Historical Museum, Wahpeton, North Dakota.

Seecof, Robert and Donna Lee Seecof. "Bookends Belong To America," *Antiques and Collecting,* March 1998, pages 36 – 37, 56 – 59.

"Seven Hundred Women Attend Pottery Open House," *Richland County Farmer-Globe,* October 22, 1940, front page.

Severy, Merle, Editor. *Wild Animals of North America.* Chicago: National Geographic Society, 1960.

Shedd, Warner. *The Kids' Wildlife Book.* Charlotte, Vermont: Williamson Publishing 1994.

Snortland, J. Signe, Editor. *A Traveler's Companion to North Dakota State Historic Sites.* Bismarck, North Dakota: State Historical Society of North Dakota, 1996.

"Souvenir Birds Prove Popular with Hunters," *Richland County Farmer-Globe,* November 6, 1945, page 1.

"Sunny Nodak Grows 'N' Grows," *North Dakotan,* October, 1957, Volume 32, Number 10, page 2.

Tarrant, Bill. *The Magic of Dogs.* New York: Lyons-Burford, 1995.

Taylor, David. *The Ultimate Dog Book.* New York; Simon and Schuster, 1990.

The Medorian, newspaper published by the Theodore Roosevelt Medora Foundation, Medora, North Dakota, Summer edition, 1998.

Theriault, Peter J. "The Jewels Stop Here," *Maine Antique Digest,* November, 1998, page 28F.

Trinka, Zena Irma. *North Dakota of Today.* St. Paul, Minnesota: Louis F. Dow Co., 1920.

Verba, Joan Marie. North Dakota, Minnesota: Lerner Company, 1992.

Wahpeton Pottery Company advertisement.

"Wahpeton Pottery Company Open House Friday," *Richland County Farmer-Globe,* October 18, 1940, front page.

"Wahpeton Only Place In Nation Selling Rosemeade Seconds," *Richland County Farmer-Globe,* May 1, 1953.

Walker, Norma J. "The Lure of the Lamp: Miller Electric Slag Glass Lamps," *Antiques and Collecting,* March 1999, Volume 104, Number 1, page 27.

Willms, Melinda Burris "A Practical Spirituality: Merchandising Mountain Handicraft," *Style 1900,* Winter/Spring, 1999, Volume 12, Number 1, pages 61 – 66.

INTERVIEWS

Althoff, Emma, North Dakota, in person, June 1999 and by telephone.

Berg, Delores, Wahpeton, North Dakota, in person, August 1972 and by telephone.

Carew, Rita Lewis, Park Rapids, Minnesota, in person, June 1999.

Dryden James, Hot Springs National Park, Arkansas, in person, August 1977 and June 1990 and by telephone May 1999.

Hektner, Olga, Wahpeton, North Dakota, in person, June 1997 and October 1998.

Kackman, Pearl, Wahpeton, North Dakota, in person, October 1998 and June 1999.

Kouba, Les, Minneapolis, Minnesota, in person, September 1998.

Lewis, Howard, Wahpeton, North Dakota, in person, August 1972, June 1989, October 1990, June 1991, and several telephone interviews.

McLaughlin, Betty, Arizona, in person, November 1995, November 1998, June 1999, and November 1999.

McLaughlin, Joe, Arizona, in person, November 1995, November 1998, June 1999, November 1999, and by telephone several times.

Mitzell, Lyle, Wahpeton, North Dakota, in person, May 1999 and June 1999.

Olson, Warren and Marge, Wahpeton, North Dakota, in person, June 1997, October 1998, and May 1999.

Radeke, Violet, Moorhead, Minnesota, in person, June 1999.

Stanley, Darel and Milli, Minneapolis, Minnesota, in person, January 2000.

ABOUT THE AUTHOR

Darlene Hurst Dommel became interested in documenting the stories of Rosemeade Pottery and its principals. She studied this pottery over a 26-year period through extensive research and "living history" — personal interviews of former employees.

Darlene Dommel, an award-winning author, holds a research-oriented master of science degree and has had over 30 years experience researching and writing about American art pottery. She has had over 50 magazine articles published in the antique field, including the first nationally published articles on eight potteries. Dommel is the author of two acclaimed books, *Collector's Encyclopedia of the Dakota Potteries*, published in 1996, and *Collector's Encyclopedia of Howard Pierce Porcelain*, published in 1998.

INDEX

INDEX

INDEX

COLLECTOR BOOKS

Informing Today's Collector

For over two decades we have been keeping collectors informed on trends and values in all fields of antiques and collectibles.

DOLLS, FIGURES & TEDDY BEARS

4707	A Decade of **Barbie** Dolls & Collectibles, 1981–1991, Summers	$19.95
4631	**Barbie** Doll Boom, 1986–1995, Augustyniak	$18.95
2079	**Barbie** Doll Fashion, Volume I, Eames	$24.95
4846	**Barbie** Doll Fashion, Volume II, Eames	$24.95
3957	**Barbie** Exclusives, Rana	$18.95
4632	**Barbie** Exclusives, Book II, Rana	$18.95
4557	**Barbie**, The First 30 Years, Deutsch	$24.95
5252	The **Barbie** Doll Years, 3rd Ed., Olds	$18.95
3810	**Chatty Cathy Dolls**, Lewis	$15.95
1529	Collector's Encyclopedia of **Barbie** Dolls, DeWein	$19.95
4882	Collector's Encyclopedia of **Barbie** Doll Exclusives and More, Augustyniak	$19.95
2211	Collector's Encyclopedia of **Madame Alexander Dolls**, Smith	$24.95
4863	Collector's Encyclopedia of **Vogue Dolls**, Izen/Stover	$29.95
3967	Collector's Guide to **Trolls**, Peterson	$19.95
5253	Story of **Barbie**, 2nd Ed., Westenhouser	$24.95
1513	**Teddy Bears & Steiff** Animals, Mandel	$9.95
1817	**Teddy Bears & Steiff** Animals, 2nd Series, Mandel	$19.95
2084	**Teddy Bears, Annalee's & Steiff** Animals, 3rd Series, Mandel	$19.95
1808	**Wonder of Barbie**, Manos	$9.95
1430	**World of Barbie** Dolls, Manos	$9.95
4880	World of **Raggedy Ann** Collectibles, Avery	$24.95

TOYS, MARBLES & CHRISTMAS COLLECTIBLES

3427	**Advertising Character** Collectibles, Dotz	$17.95
2333	Antique & Collector's **Marbles**, 3rd Ed., Grist	$9.95
4934	**Breyer Animal** Collector's Guide, Identification and Values, Browell	$19.95
4976	**Christmas** Ornaments, Lights & Decorations, Johnson	$24.95
4737	**Christmas** Ornaments, Lights & Decorations, Vol. II, Johnson	$24.95
4739	**Christmas** Ornaments, Lights & Decorations, Vol. III, Johnson	$24.95
4649	Classic Plastic **Model Kits**, Polizzi	$24.95
4559	Collectible **Action Figures**, 2nd Ed., Manos	$17.95
3874	Collectible Coca-Cola Toy **Trucks**, deCourtivron	$24.95
2338	Collector's Encyclopedia of **Disneyana**, Longest, Stern	$24.95
4958	Collector's Guide to **Battery Toys**, Hultzman	$19.95
5038	Collector's Guide to **Diecast Toys & Scale Models**, 2nd Ed., Johnson	$19.95
4651	Collector's Guide to **Tinker Toys**, Strange	$18.95
4566	Collector's Guide to **Tootsietoys**, 2nd Ed., Richter	$19.95
5169	Collector's Guide to **TV Toys** & Memorabilia, 2nd Ed., Davis/Morgan	$24.95
4720	The Golden Age of **Automotive Toys**, 1925–1941, Hutchison/Johnson	$24.95
3436	Grist's Big Book of **Marbles**	$19.95
3970	Grist's Machine-Made & Contemporary **Marbles**, 2nd Ed.	$9.95
5267	**Matchbox** Toys, 1947 to 1998, 3rd Ed., Johnson	$19.95
4871	**McDonald's Collectibles**, Henriques/DuVall	$19.95
1540	**Modern Toys** 1930–1980, Baker	$19.95
3888	**Motorcycle** Toys, Antique & Contemporary, Gentry/Downs	$18.95
5168	Schroeder's Collectible **Toys**, Antique to Modern Price Guide, 5th Ed.	$17.95
1886	Stern's Guide to **Disney** Collectibles	$14.95
2139	Stern's Guide to **Disney** Collectibles, 2nd Series	$14.95
3975	Stern's Guide to **Disney** Collectibles, 3rd Series	$18.95
2028	**Toys**, Antique & Collectible, Longest	$14.95

FURNITURE

1457	American **Oak** Furniture, McNerney	$9.95
3716	American **Oak** Furniture, Book II, McNerney	$12.95
1118	Antique **Oak** Furniture, Hill	$7.95
2271	Collector's Encyclopedia of **American** Furniture, Vol. II, Swedberg	$24.95
3720	Collector's Encyclopedia of **American** Furniture, Vol. III, Swedberg	$24.95
1755	Furniture of the **Depression Era**, Swedberg	$19.95
3906	**Heywood-Wakefield** Modern Furniture, Rouland	$18.95
1885	**Victorian** Furniture, Our American Heritage, McNerney	$9.95
3829	**Victorian** Furniture, Our American Heritage, Book II, McNerney	$9.95

JEWELRY, HATPINS, WATCHES & PURSES

1712	Antique & Collector's **Thimbles** & Accessories, Mathis	$19.95
1748	Antique **Purses**, Revised Second Ed., Holiner	$19.95
1278	Art Nouveau & Art Deco **Jewelry**, Baker	$9.95
4850	Collectible **Costume Jewelry**, Simonds	$24.95
3875	Collecting Antique **Stickpins**, Kerins	$16.95
3722	Collector's Ency. of **Compacts, Carryalls & Face Powder Boxes**, Mueller	$24.95
4854	Collector's Ency. of **Compacts, Carryalls & Face Powder Boxes**, Vol. II	$24.95
4940	**Costume Jewelry**, A Practical Handbook & Value Guide, Rezazadeh	$24.95
1716	Fifty Years of Collectible **Fashion Jewelry**, 1925–1975, Baker	$19.95
1424	**Hatpins** & Hatpin Holders, Baker	$9.95
1181	100 Years of Collectible **Jewelry**, 1850–1950, Baker	$9.95
4729	**Sewing Tools** & Trinkets, Thompson	$24.95
4878	Vintage & Contemporary **Purse Accessories**, Gerson	$24.95
3830	Vintage **Vanity Bags & Purses**, Gerson	$24.95

INDIANS, GUNS, KNIVES, TOOLS, PRIMITIVES

1868	Antique **Tools**, Our American Heritage, McNerney	$9.95
1426	**Arrowheads** & Projectile Points, Hothem	$7.95
4943	Field Guide to **Flint Arrowheads & Knives** of the North American Indian	$9.95
2279	**Indian Artifacts** of the Midwest, Hothem	$14.95
3885	**Indian Artifacts** of the Midwest, Book II, Hothem	$16.95
4870	**Indian Artifacts** of the Midwest, Book III, Hothem	$18.95
5162	Modern **Guns**, Identification & Values, 12th Ed., Quertermous	$12.95
2164	**Primitives**, Our American Heritage, McNerney	$9.95
1759	**Primitives**, Our American Heritage, 2nd Series, McNerney	$14.95
4730	Standard **Knife** Collector's Guide, 3rd Ed., Ritchie & Stewart	$12.95

PAPER COLLECTIBLES & BOOKS

4633	**Big Little Books**, Jacobs	$18.95
4710	Collector's Guide to **Children's Books**, 1850 to 1950, Jones	$18.95
1441	Collector's Guide to **Post Cards**, Wood	$9.95
2081	Guide to Collecting **Cookbooks**, Allen	$14.95
5271	Huxford's **Old Book** Value Guide, 11th Ed.	$19.95
2080	Price Guide to **Cookbooks** & Recipe Leaflets, Dickinson	$9.95
3973	**Sheet Music** Reference & Price Guide, 2nd Ed., Pafik & Guiheen	$19.95
4654	**Victorian Trade Cards**, Historical Reference & Value Guide, Cheadle	$19.95
4733	**Whitman Juvenile Books**, Brown	$17.95

GLASSWARE

4561	Collectible **Drinking Glasses**, Chase & Kelly	$17.95
4642	Collectible **Glass Shoes**, Wheatley	$19.95
4937	Coll. **Glassware** from the 40s, 50s & 60s, 4th Ed., Florence	$19.95
1810	Collector's Encyclopedia of **American Art Glass**, Shuman	$29.95
4938	Collector's Encyclopedia of **Depression Glass**, 13th Ed., Florence	$19.95
1961	Collector's Encyclopedia of **Fry Glassware**, Fry Glass Society	$24.95
1664	Collector's Encyclopedia of **Heisey Glass**, 1925–1938, Bredehoft	$24.95
3905	Collector's Encyclopedia of **Milk Glass**, Newbound	$24.95
4936	Collector's Guide to **Candy Containers**, Dezso/Poirier	$19.95
4564	**Crackle Glass**, Weitman	$19.95
4941	**Crackle Glass**, Book II, Weitman	$19.95
4714	**Czechoslovakian Glass** and Collectibles, Book II, Barta/Rose	$16.95
5158	**Elegant Glassware** of the Depression Era, 8th Ed., Florence	$19.95
1380	Encyclopedia of **Pattern Glass**, McCain	$12.95
3981	Evers' Standard **Cut Glass** Value Guide	$12.95
4659	**Fenton Art Glass**, 1907–1939, Whitmyer	$24.95
3725	**Fostoria**, Pressed, Blown & Hand Molded Shapes, Kerr	$24.95
4719	**Fostoria**, Etched, Carved & Cut Designs, Vol. II, Kerr	$24.95
3883	**Fostoria Stemware**, The Crystal for America, Long & Seate	$24.95
4644	**Imperial Carnival Glass**, Burns	$18.95
3886	**Kitchen Glassware** of the Depression Years, 5th Ed., Florence	$19.95
5156	Pocket Guide to **Depression Glass**, 11th Ed., Florence	$9.95

COLLECTOR BOOKS
Informing Today's Collector

5035	Standard Encyclopedia of **Carnival Glass**, 6th Ed., Edwards/Carwile	$24.95
5036	Standard **Carnival Glass** Price Guide, 11th Ed., Edwards/Carwile	$9.95
5272	Standard Encyclopedia of **Opalescent Glass**, 3rd ed., Edwards	$24.95
4731	**Stemware Identification**, Featuring Cordials with Values, Florence	$24.95
3326	**Very Rare Glassware** of the Depression Years, 3rd Series, Florence	$24.95
4732	**Very Rare Glassware** of the Depression Years, 5th Series, Florence	$24.95
4656	**Westmoreland Glass**, Wilson	$24.95

POTTERY

4927	**ABC Plates & Mugs**, Lindsay	$24.95
4929	**American Art Pottery**, Sigafoose	$24.95
4630	**American Limoges**, Limoges	$24.95
1312	**Blue & White Stoneware**, McNerney	$9.95
1958	So. Potteries **Blue Ridge Dinnerware**, 3rd Ed., Newbound	$14.95
1959	**Blue Willow**, 2nd Ed., Gaston	$14.95
4848	Ceramic **Coin Banks**, Stoddard	$19.95
4851	Collectible **Cups & Saucers**, Harran	$18.95
4709	Collectible **Kay Finch**, Biography, Identification & Values, Martinez/Frick	$18.95
1373	Collector's Encyclopedia of **American Dinnerware**, Cunningham	$24.95
4931	Collector's Encyclopedia of **Bauer Pottery**, Chipman	$24.95
4932	Collector's Encyclopedia of **Blue Ridge Dinnerware**, Vol. II, Newbound	$24.95
4658	Collector's Encyclopedia of **Brush-McCoy Pottery**, Huxford	$24.95
5034	Collector's Encyclopedia of **California Pottery**, 2nd Ed., Chipman	$24.95
2133	Collector's Encyclopedia of **Cookie Jars**, Roerig	$24.95
3723	Collector's Encyclopedia of **Cookie Jars**, Book II, Roerig	$24.95
4939	Collector's Encyclopedia of **Cookie Jars**, Book III, Roerig	$24.95
4638	Collector's Encyclopedia of **Dakota Potteries**, Dommel	$24.95
5040	Collector's Encyclopedia of **Fiesta**, 8th Ed., Huxford	$19.95
4718	Collector's Encyclopedia of **Figural Planters & Vases**, Newbound	$19.95
3961	Collector's Encyclopedia of **Early Noritake**, Alden	$24.95
1439	Collector's Encyclopedia of **Flow Blue China**, Gaston	$19.95
3812	Collector's Encyclopedia of **Flow Blue China**, 2nd Ed., Gaston	$24.95
3813	Collector's Encyclopedia of **Hall China**, 2nd Ed., Whitmyer	$24.95
3431	Collector's Encyclopedia of **Homer Laughlin China**, Jasper	$24.95
1276	Collector's Encyclopedia of **Hull Pottery**, Roberts	$19.95
3962	Collector's Encyclopedia of **Lefton China**, DeLozier	$19.95
4855	Collector's Encyclopedia of **Lefton China**, Book II, DeLozier	$19.95
2210	Collector's Encyclopedia of **Limoges Porcelain**, 2nd Ed., Gaston	$24.95
2334	Collector's Encyclopedia of **Majolica Pottery**, Katz-Marks	$19.95
1358	Collector's Encyclopedia of **McCoy Pottery**, Huxford	$19.95
3963	Collector's Encyclopedia of **Metlox Potteries**, Gibbs Jr.	$24.95
3837	Collector's Encyclopedia of **Nippon Porcelain**, Van Patten	$24.95
2089	Collector's Ency. of **Nippon Porcelain**, 2nd Series, Van Patten	$24.95
1665	Collector's Ency. of **Nippon Porcelain**, 3rd Series, Van Patten	$24.95
4712	Collector's Ency. of **Nippon Porcelain**, 4th Series, Van Patten	$24.95
1447	Collector's Encyclopedia of **Noritake**, Van Patten	$19.95
1037	Collector's Encyclopedia of **Occupied Japan**, 1st Series, Florence	$14.95
1038	Collector's Encyclopedia of **Occupied Japan**, 2nd Series, Florence	$14.95
2088	Collector's Encyclopedia of **Occupied Japan**, 3rd Series, Florence	$14.95
2019	Collector's Encyclopedia of **Occupied Japan**, 4th Series, Florence	$14.95
2335	Collector's Encyclopedia of **Occupied Japan**, 5th Series, Florence	$14.95
4951	Collector's Encyclopedia of **Old Ivory China**, Hillman	$24.95
3964	Collector's Encyclopedia of **Pickard China**, Reed	$24.95
3877	Collector's Encyclopedia of **R.S. Prussia**, 4th Series, Gaston	$24.95
1034	Collector's Encyclopedia of **Roseville Pottery**, Huxford	$19.95
1035	Collector's Encyclopedia of **Roseville Pottery**, 2nd Ed., Huxford	$19.95
4856	Collector's Encyclopedia of **Russel Wright**, 2nd Ed., Kerr	$24.95
4713	Collector's Encyclopedia of **Salt Glaze Stoneware**, Taylor/Lowrance	$24.95
3314	Collector's Encyclopedia of **Van Briggle** Art Pottery, Sasicki	$24.95
4563	Collector's Encyclopedia of **Wall Pockets**, Newbound	$19.95
2111	Collector's Encyclopedia of **Weller Pottery**, Huxford	$29.95
3876	Collector's Guide to **Lu-Ray Pastels**, Meehan	$18.95
3814	Collector's Guide to **Made in Japan** Ceramics, White	$18.95
4646	Collector's Guide to **Made in Japan** Ceramics, Book II, White	$18.95
2339	Collector's Guide to **Shawnee Pottery**, Vanderbilt	$19.95

1425	**Cookie Jars**, Westfall	$9.95
3440	**Cookie Jars**, Book II, Westfall	$19.95
4924	Figural & Novelty **Salt & Pepper Shakers**, 2nd Series, Davern	$24.95
2379	Lehner's Ency. of **U.S. Marks** on Pottery, Porcelain & China	$24.95
4722	**McCoy Pottery**, Collector's Reference & Value Guide, Hanson/Nissen	$19.95
4726	**Red Wing Art Pottery**, 1920s–1960s, Dollen	$19.95
1670	**Red Wing Collectibles**, DePasquale	$9.95
1440	**Red Wing Stoneware**, DePasquale	$9.95
1632	**Salt & Pepper Shakers**, Guarnaccia	$9.95
5091	**Salt & Pepper Shakers** II, Guarnaccia	$18.95
2220	**Salt & Pepper Shakers** III, Guarnaccia	$14.95
3443	**Salt & Pepper Shakers** IV, Guarnaccia	$18.95
3738	**Shawnee Pottery**, Mangus	$24.95
4629	Turn of the Century **American Dinnerware**, 1880s–1920s, Jasper	$24.95
3327	**Watt Pottery** – Identification & Value Guide, Morris	$19.95

OTHER COLLECTIBLES

4704	Antique & Collectible **Buttons**, Wisniewski	$19.95
2269	Antique **Brass & Copper** Collectibles, Gaston	$16.95
1880	Antique **Iron**, McNerney	$9.95
3872	Antique **Tins**, Dodge	$24.95
4845	Antique **Typewriters & Office Collectibles**, Rehr	$19.95
1714	**Black** Collectibles, Gibbs	$19.95
1128	**Bottle** Pricing Guide, 3rd Ed., Cleveland	$7.95
4636	**Celluloid Collectibles**, Dunn	$14.95
3718	Collectible **Aluminum**, Grist	$16.95
4560	Collectible **Cats**, An Identification & Value Guide, Book II, Fyke	$19.95
4852	Collectible **Compact Disc** Price Guide 2, Cooper	$17.95
2018	Collector's Encyclopedia of **Granite Ware**, Greguire	$24.95
3430	Collector's Encyclopedia of **Granite Ware**, Book 2, Greguire	$24.95
4705	Collector's Guide to **Antique Radios**, 4th Ed., Bunis	$18.95
3880	Collector's Guide to **Cigarette Lighters**, Flanagan	$17.95
4637	Collector's Guide to **Cigarette Lighters**, Book II, Flanagan	$17.95
4942	Collector's Guide to **Don Winton Designs**, Ellis	$19.95
3966	Collector's Guide to **Inkwells**, Identification & Values, Badders	$18.95
4947	Collector's Guide to **Inkwells**, Book II, Badders	$19.95
4948	Collector's Guide to **Letter Openers**, Grist	$19.95
4862	Collector's Guide to **Toasters** & Accessories, Greguire	$19.95
4652	Collector's Guide to **Transistor Radios**, 2nd Ed., Bunis	$16.95
4864	Collector's Guide to **Wallace Nutting Pictures**, Ivankovich	$18.95
1629	**Doorstops**, Identification & Values, Bertoia	$9.95
4567	Figural **Napkin Rings**, Gottschalk & Whitson	$18.95
4717	Figural **Nodders**, Includes Bobbin' Heads and Swayers, Irtz	$19.95
3968	**Fishing Lure** Collectibles, Murphy/Edmisten	$24.95
5259	**Flea Market Trader**, 12th Ed., Huxford	$9.95
4944	**Flue Covers**, Collector's Value Guide, Meckley	$12.95
4945	**G-Men and FBI Toys** and Collectibles, Whitworth	$18.95
5263	**Garage Sale & Flea Market Annual**, 7th Ed.	$19.95
3819	**General Store Collectibles**, Wilson	$24.95
5159	Huxford's Collectible **Advertising**, 4th Ed.	$24.95
2216	**Kitchen Antiques**, 1790–1940, McNerney	$14.95
4950	The **Lone Ranger**, Collector's Reference & Value Guide, Felbinger	$18.95
2026	**Railroad** Collectibles, 4th Ed., Baker	$14.95
5167	**Schroeder's Antiques Price Guide**, 17th Ed., Huxford	$12.95
5007	**Silverplated Flatware**, Revised 4th Edition, Hagan	$18.95
1922	Standard **Old Bottle** Price Guide, Sellari	$14.95
5154	**Summers' Guide to Coca-Cola**, 2nd Ed.	$19.95
4952	**Summers' Pocket Guide to Coca-Cola** Identifications	$9.95
3892	**Toy & Miniature Sewing Machines**, Thomas	$18.95
4876	**Toy & Miniature Sewing Machines**, Book II, Thomas	$24.95
5144	**Value Guide to Advertising Memorabilia**, 2nd Ed., Summers	$19.95
3977	**Value Guide to Gas Station** Memorabilia, Summers & Priddy	$24.95
4877	**Vintage Bar Ware**, Visakay	$24.95
4935	The **W.F. Cody Buffalo Bill** Collector's Guide with Values	$24.95
5281	**Wanted to Buy**, 7th Edition	$9.95

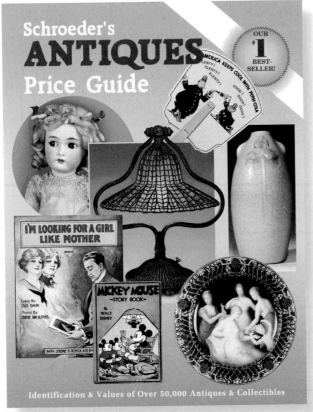